THE ANALOG CAMERA

Looking Back

The Analog Camera

Looking Back

Wolf Arnold

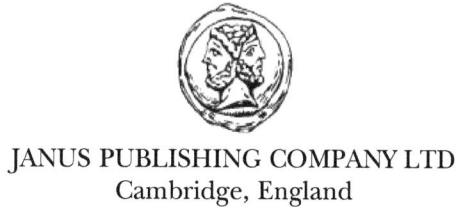

JANUS PUBLISHING COMPANY LTD
Cambridge, England

First published in Great Britain 2016
by Janus Publishing Company Ltd
The Studio High Green
Great Shelford
Cambridge CB22 5EG

www.januspublishing.co.uk

British Library Cataloguing-in-Publication Data
A catalogue record for this book is available from the British Library

ISBN 978-1-85756-854-7

Cover Design: Janus Publishing

Front cover image: A railroad station, Barcelona, Spain
Back cover image: Gargoyle, Notre-Dame Cathedral, Paris
Both images were supplied by the Author

If any person recognises themselves in a photograph, I apologise for using this image without their permission.

Printed and bound in Great Britain

Introduction

Some pictures are worth a thousand words, so the story goes. Others tell a story, or better, should tell a story. The people the camera snaps in an instant have a story to tell. They have plans, ambitions, dreams, have experienced hardships, have a life before them or a life well lived. They and the photographs of them are unique. We should respect them.

Buildings, streets and situations also have a story to tell. Two images of Berlin, however nondescript, stand out. The picture of the station with the name Charlottenburg, bleak and run-down, is actually in former West Berlin, which by then in the 1950s was steadily improving after the war. But the city's commuter-train system, part of the former Reichsbahn, the state railroad, was administered by the East German regime, a situation typical of the oddities in a city occupied by four powers and divided by two ideologies.

The shot of the elevated Metro and the double-decker bus tells another story. Here we see the scars of war and a new modern bus, the bus a product of a new era when Marshall Plan funds (the European Recovery Programme) were helping to rebuild the city; its damaged infrastructure, in part, still had to wait.

Take a look at the picture of the man filling up his Volkswagen. He could be a retired civil servant or a tool-and-die maker, content with his present situation. The car, from its humble beginnings, when you needed a wooden stick to measure how much petrol you still had in the tank, embodies the rise of an economy and social order from ashes to prosperity, thanks to people like the man in the photo.

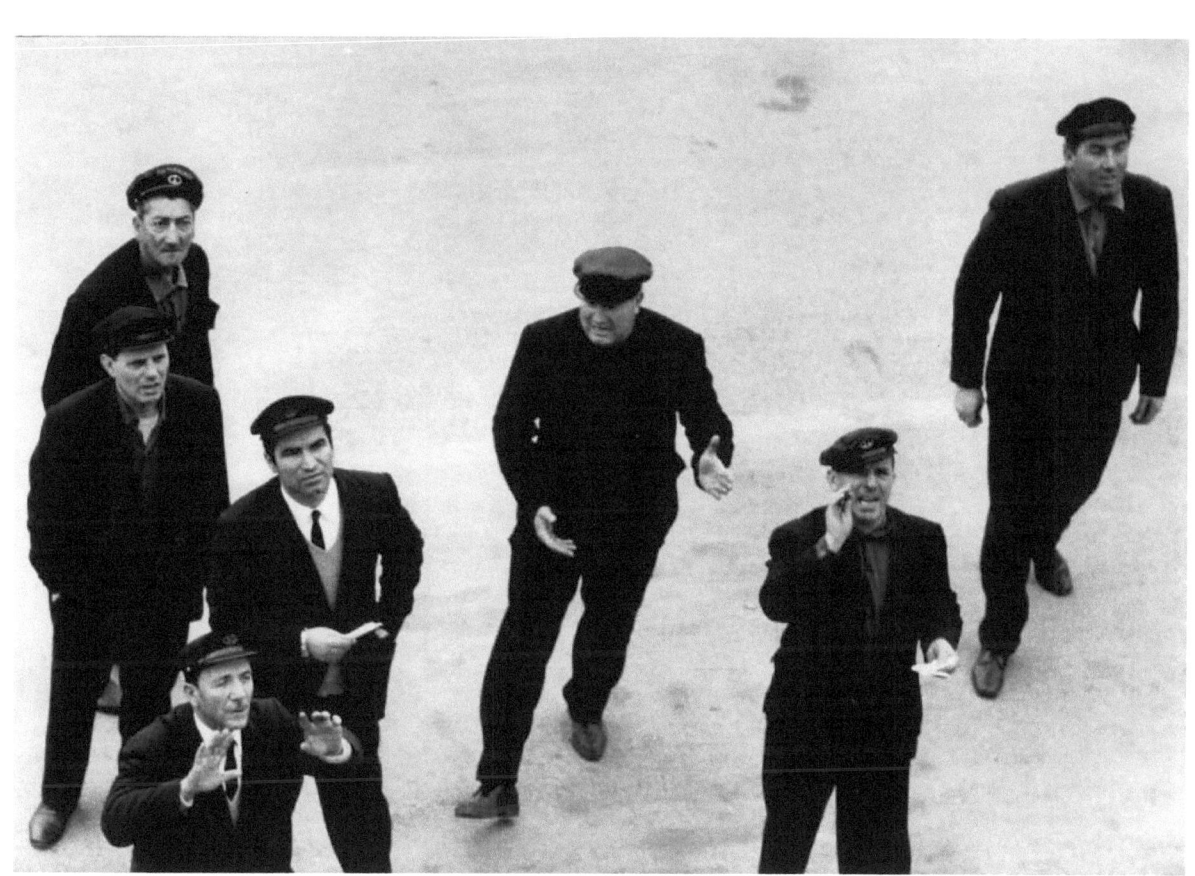

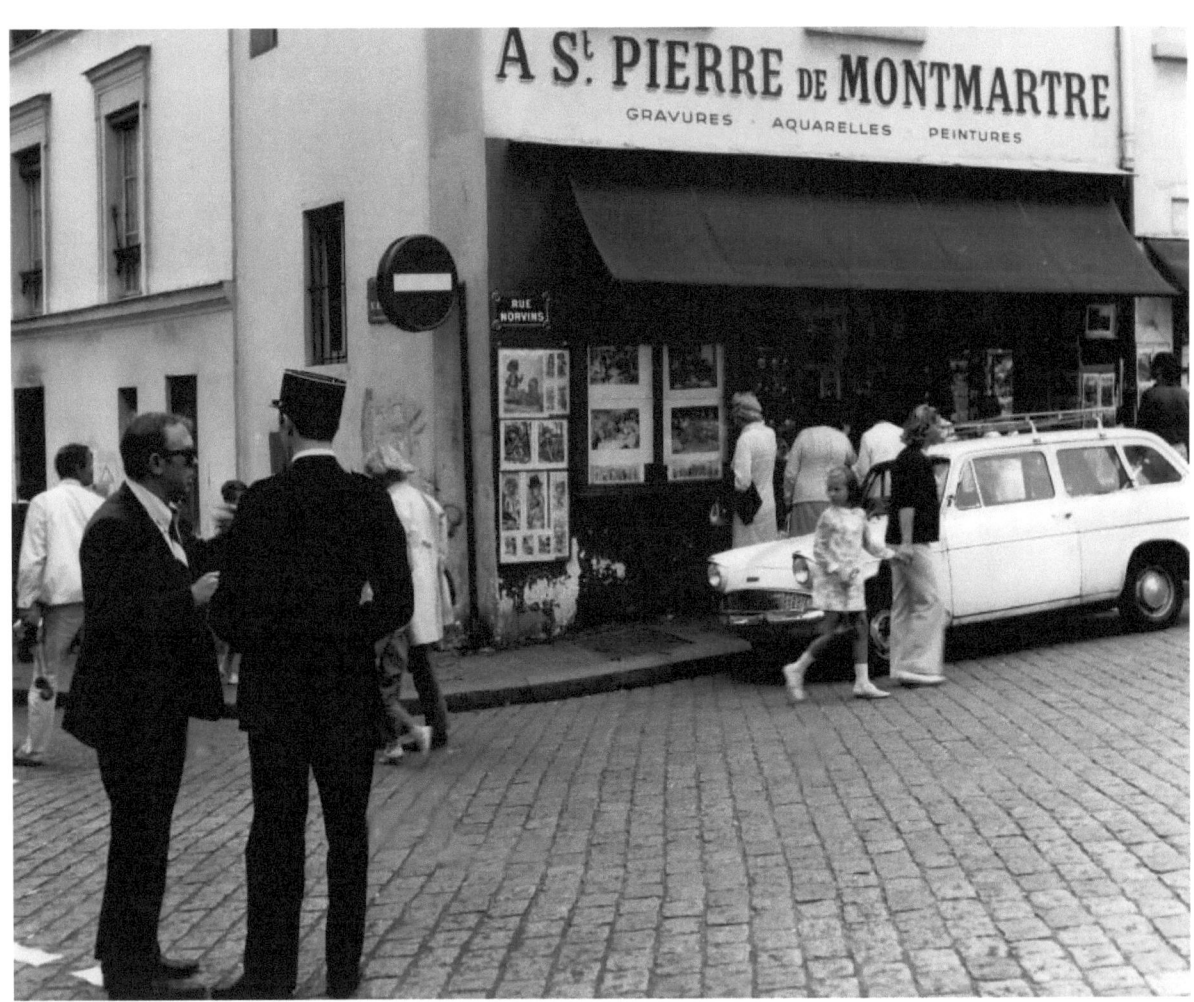

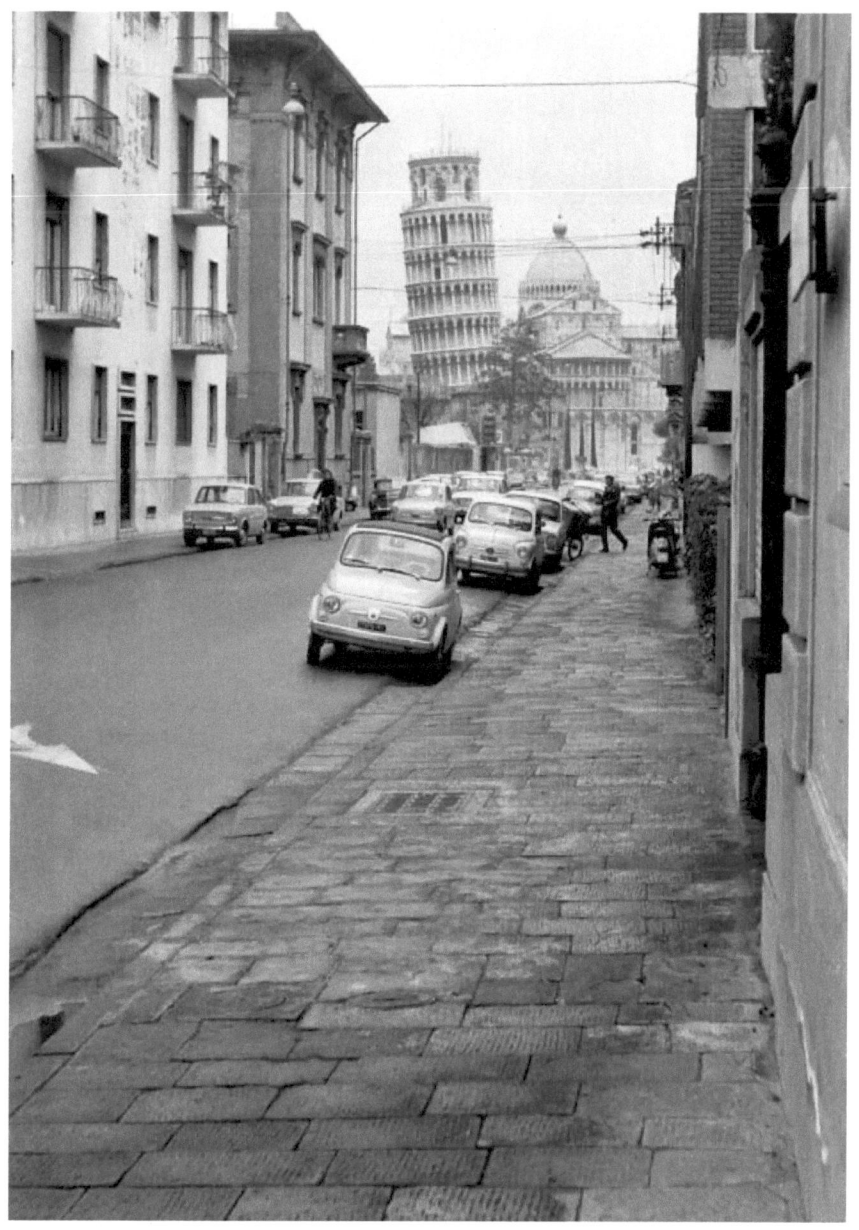

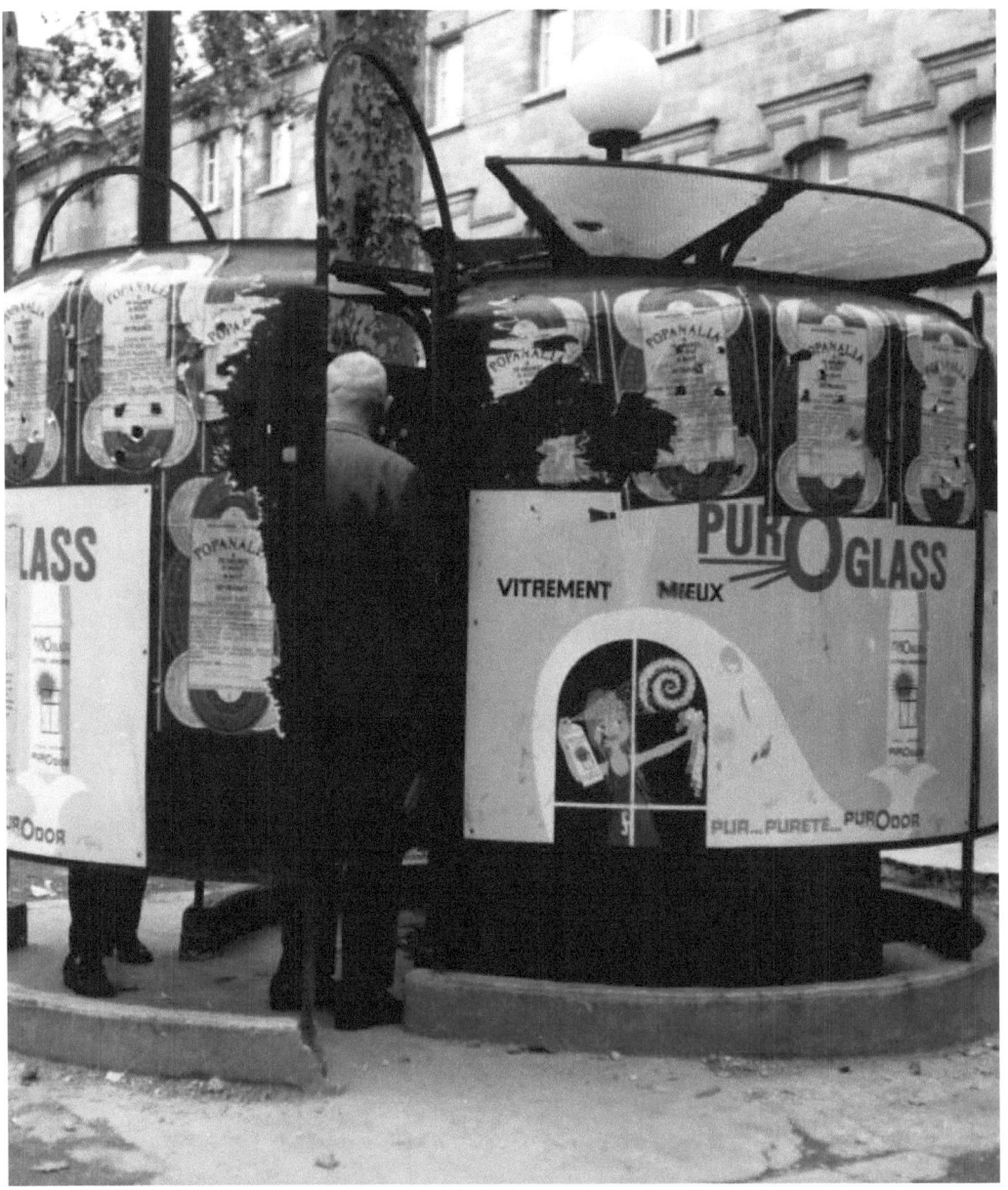

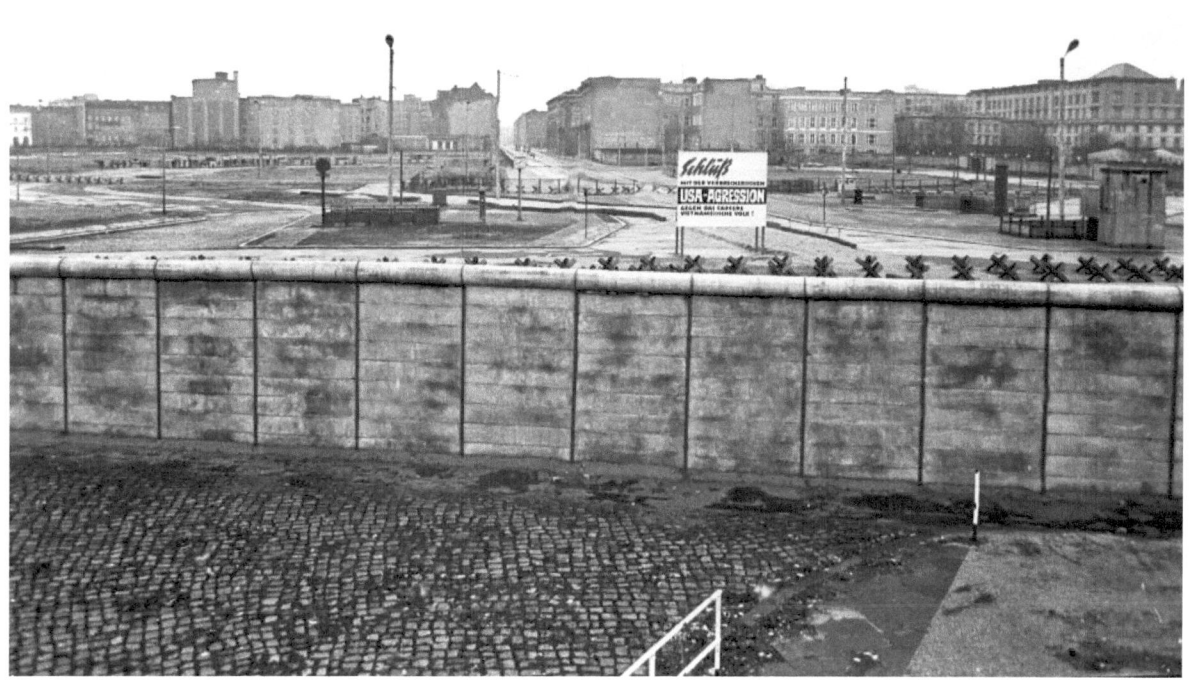

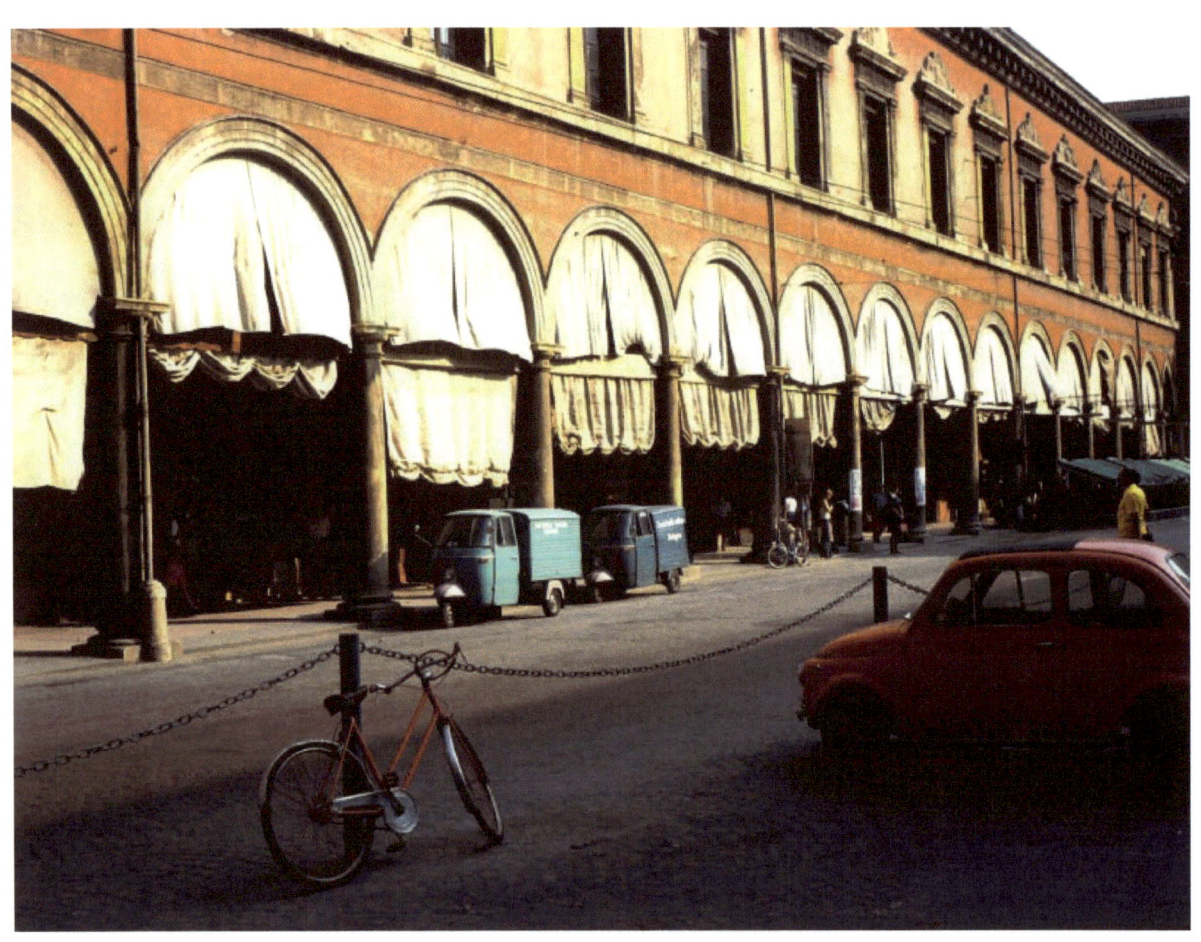

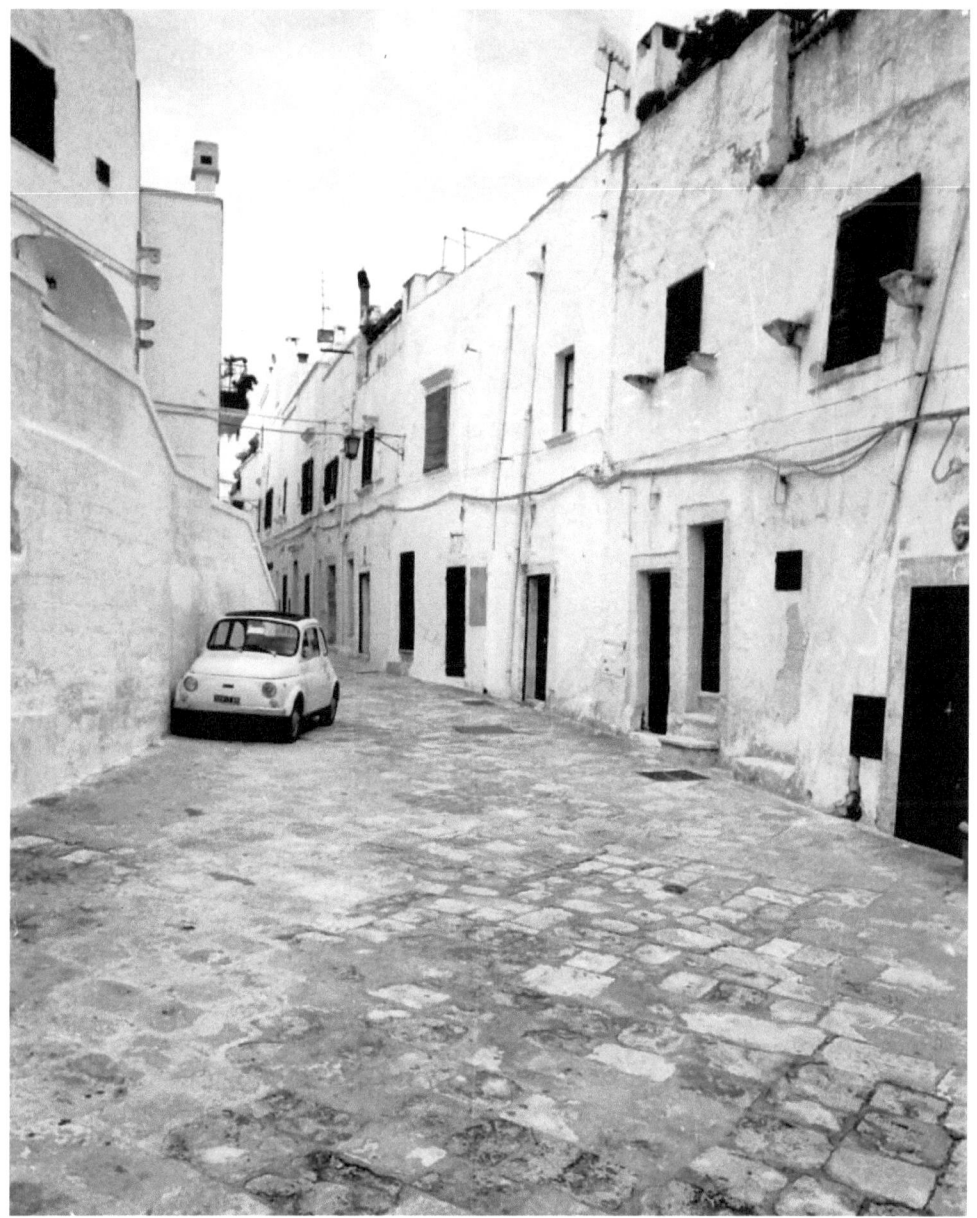

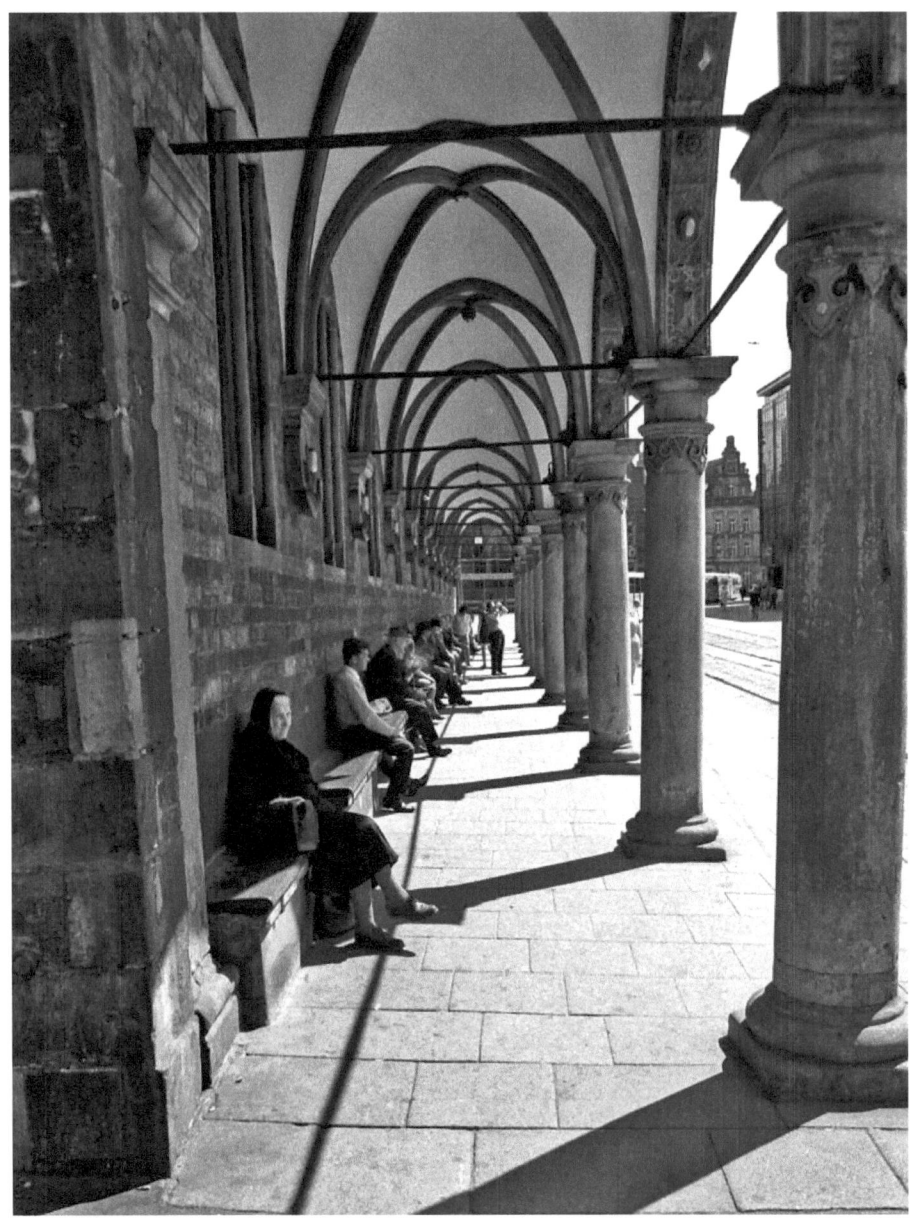

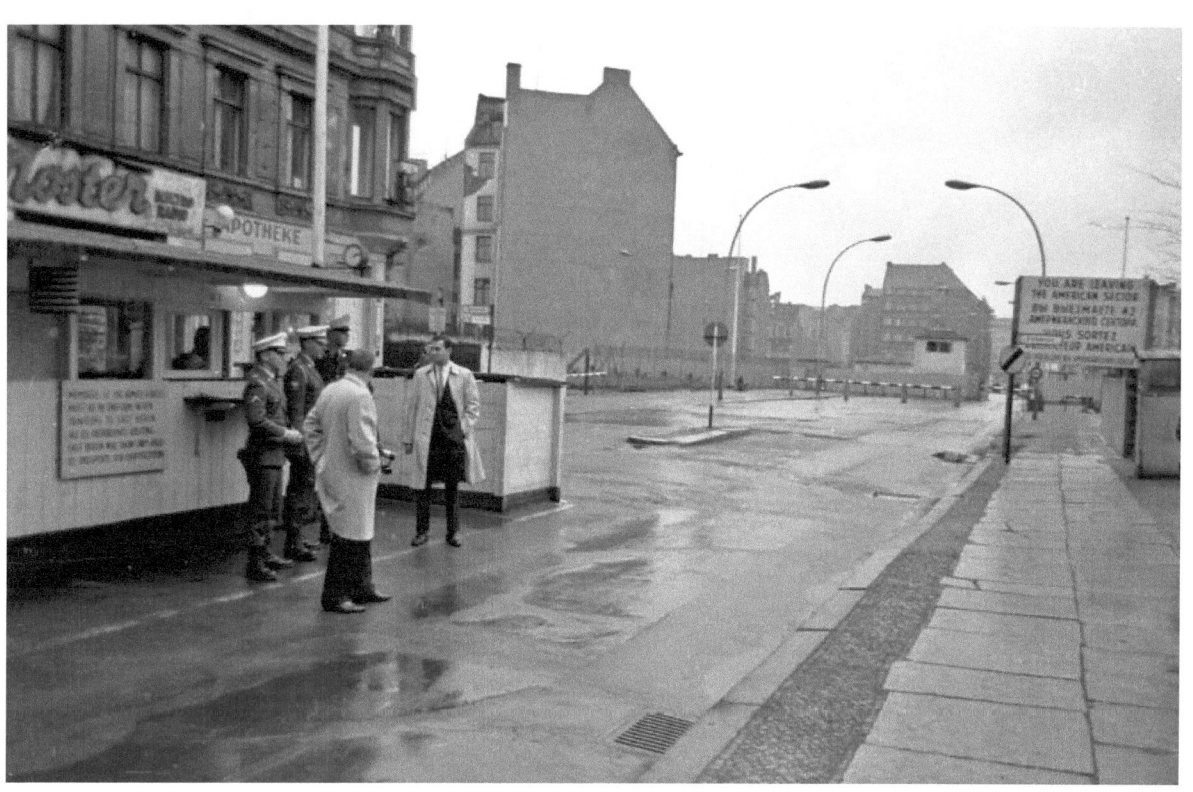

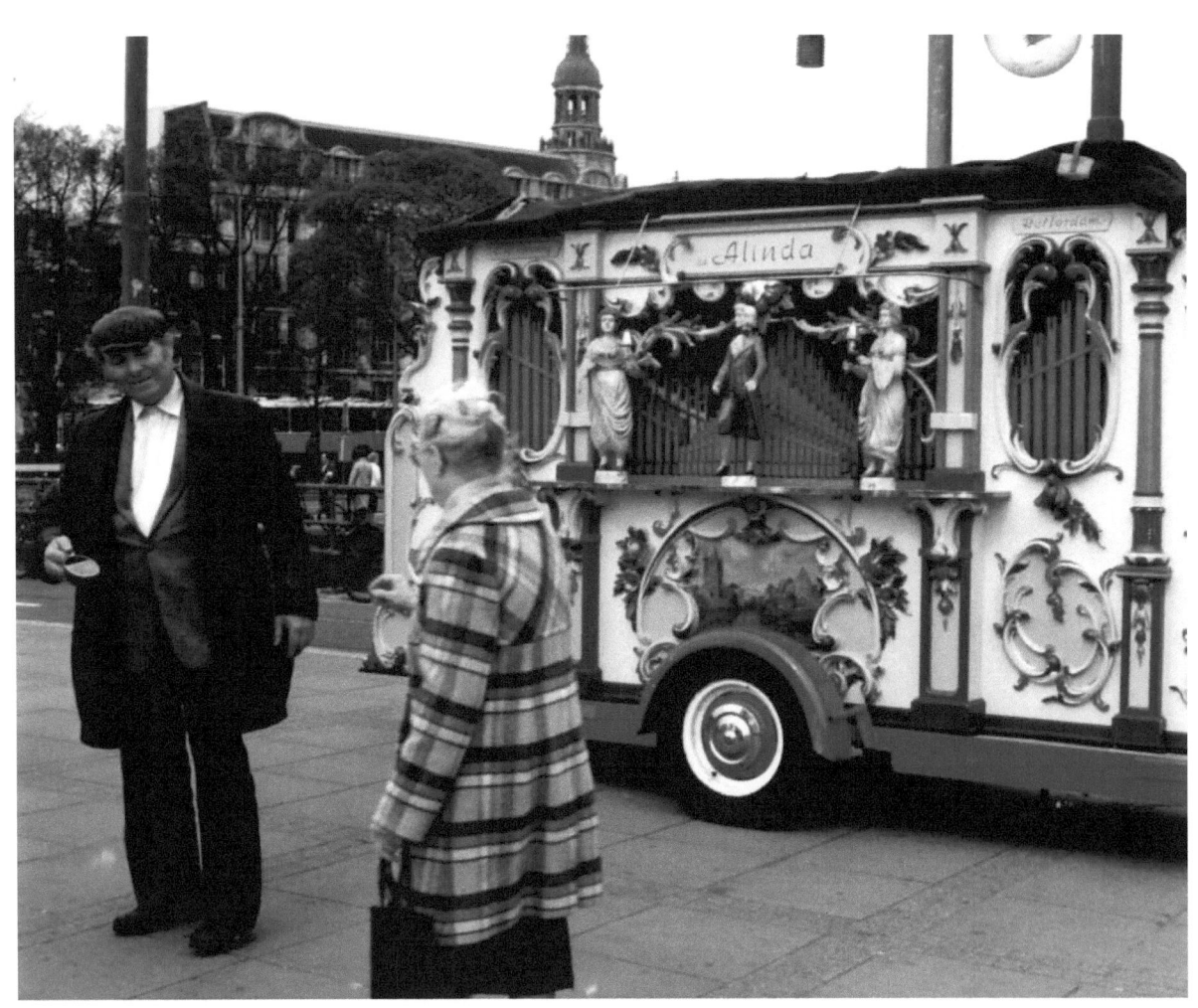

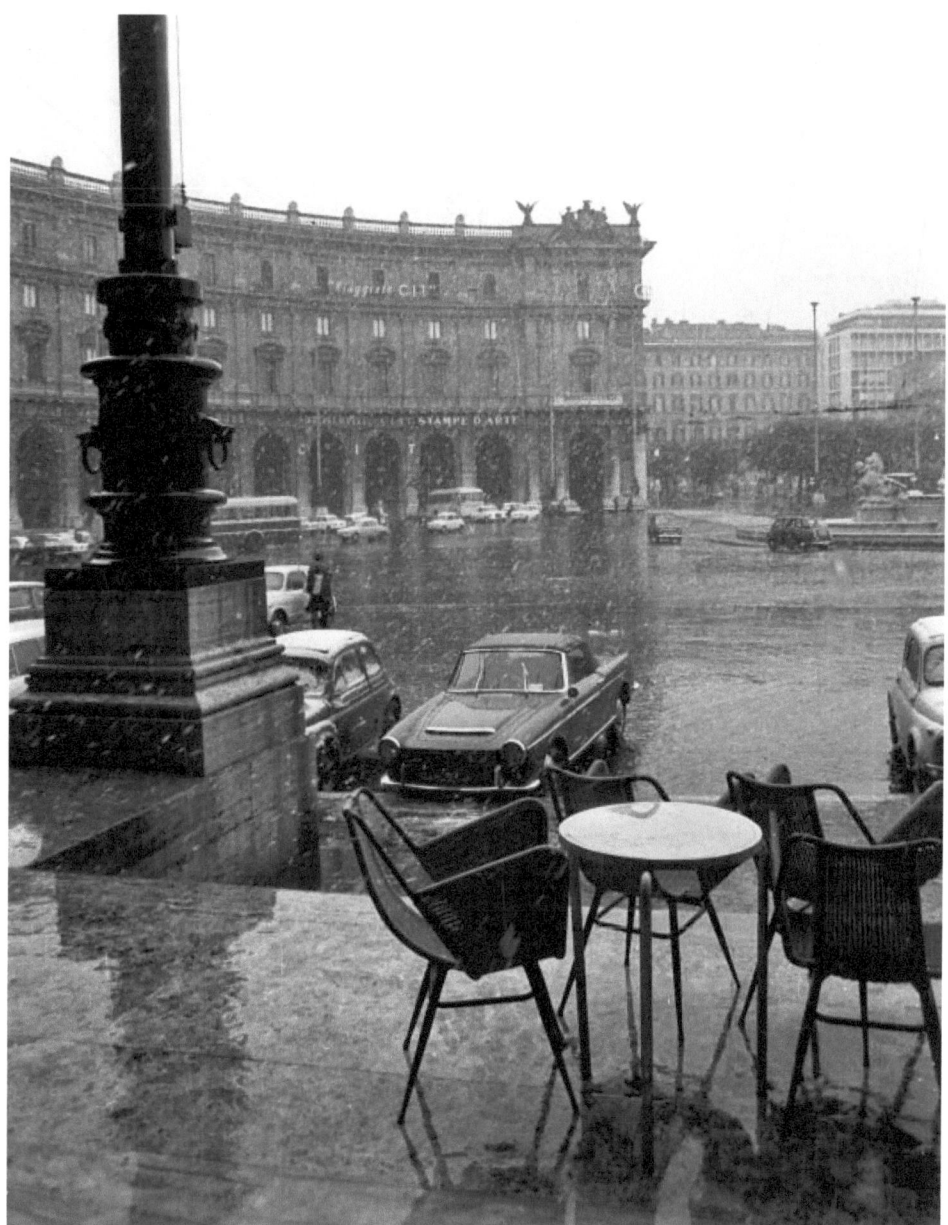

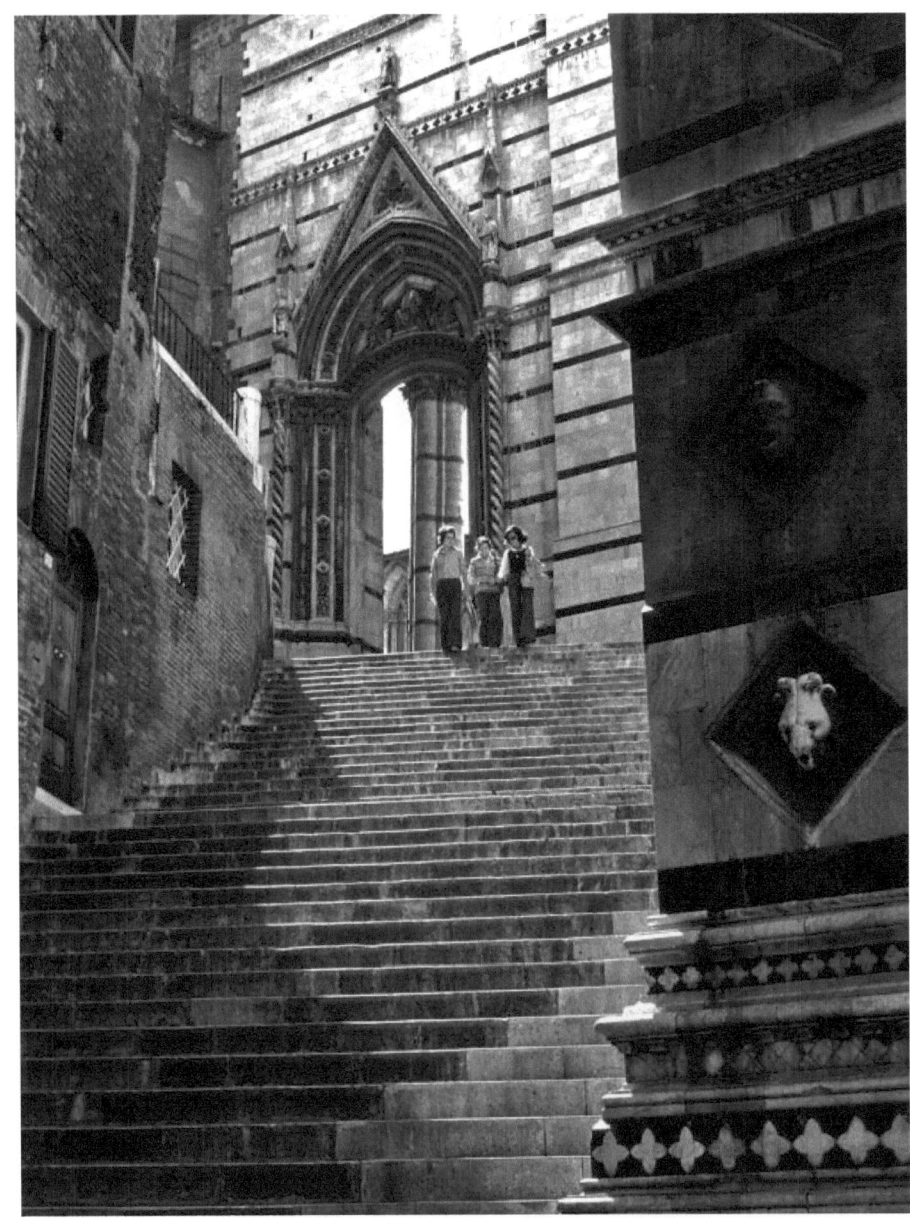

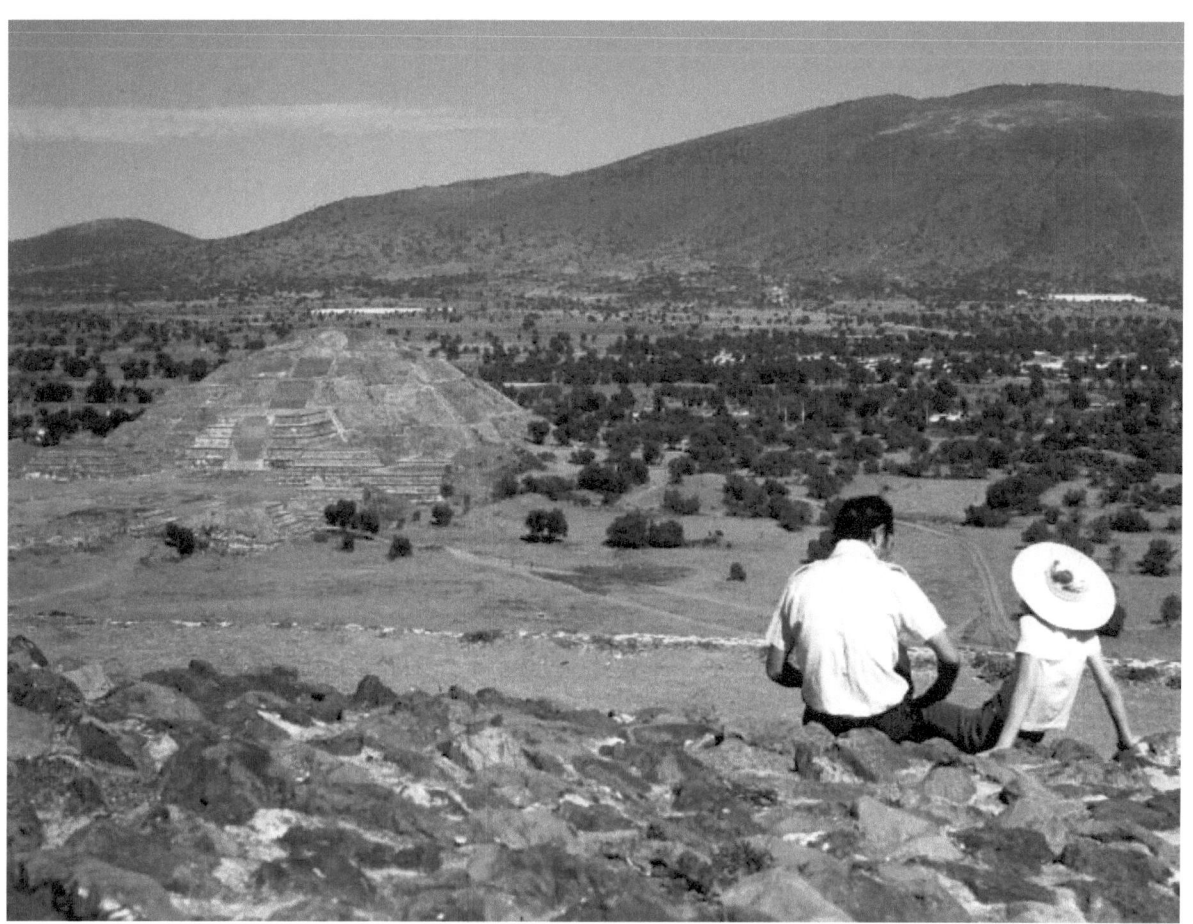

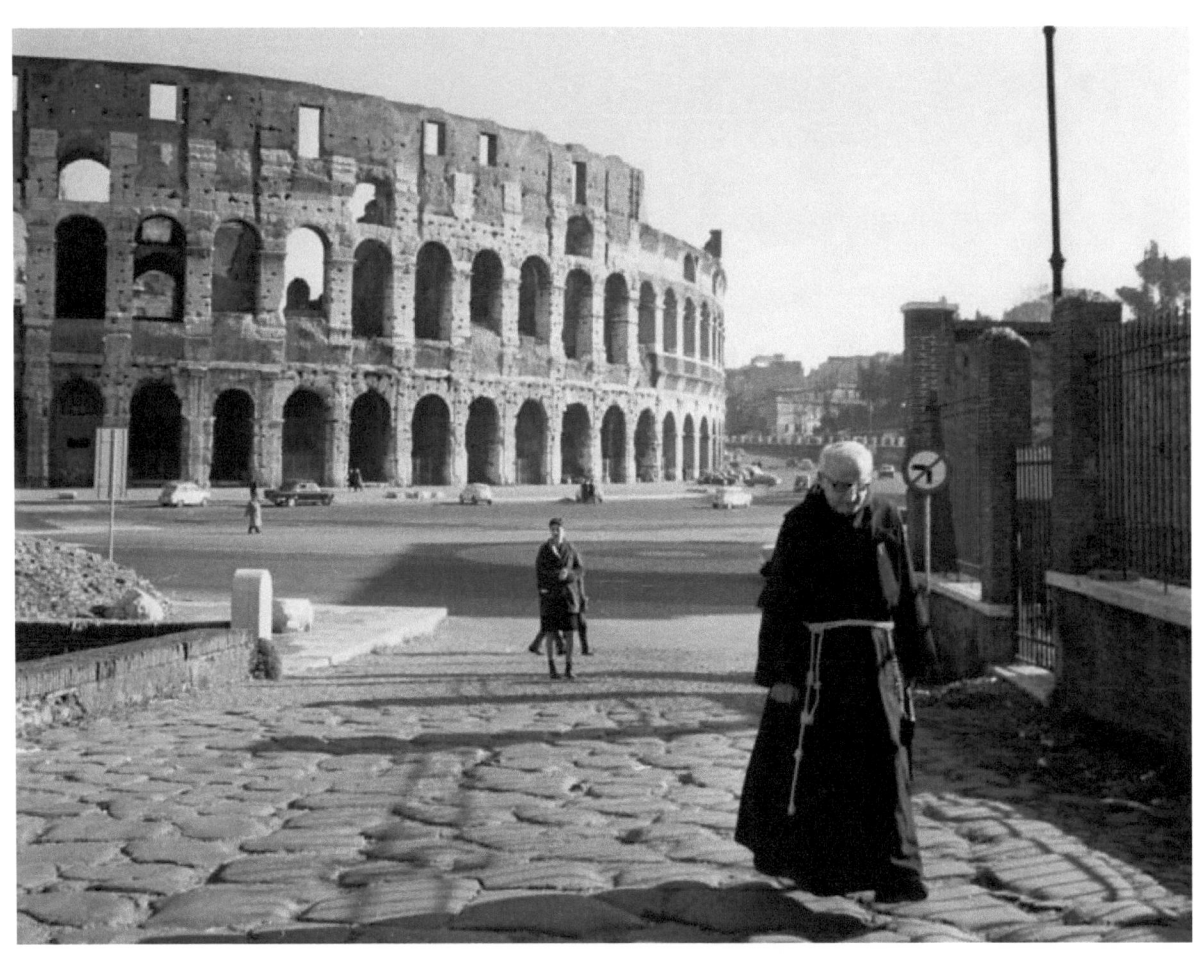

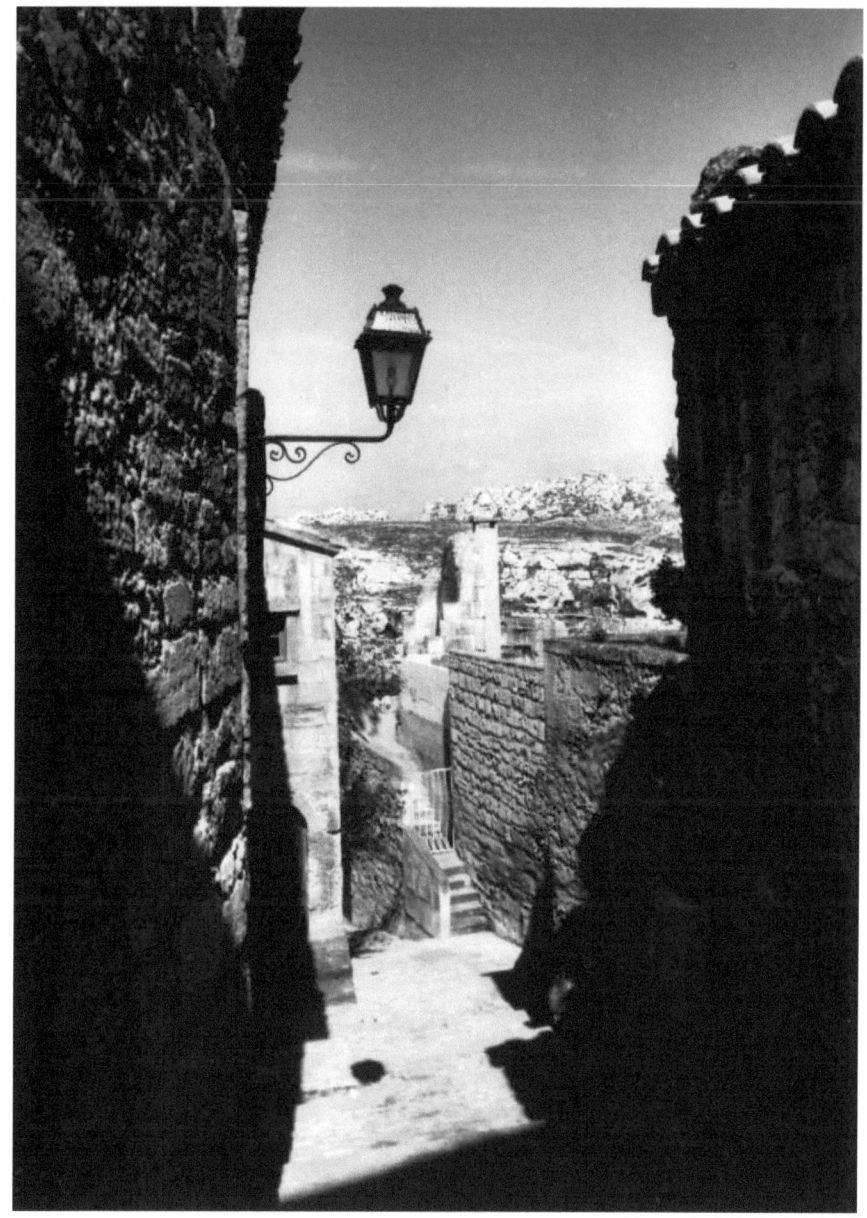

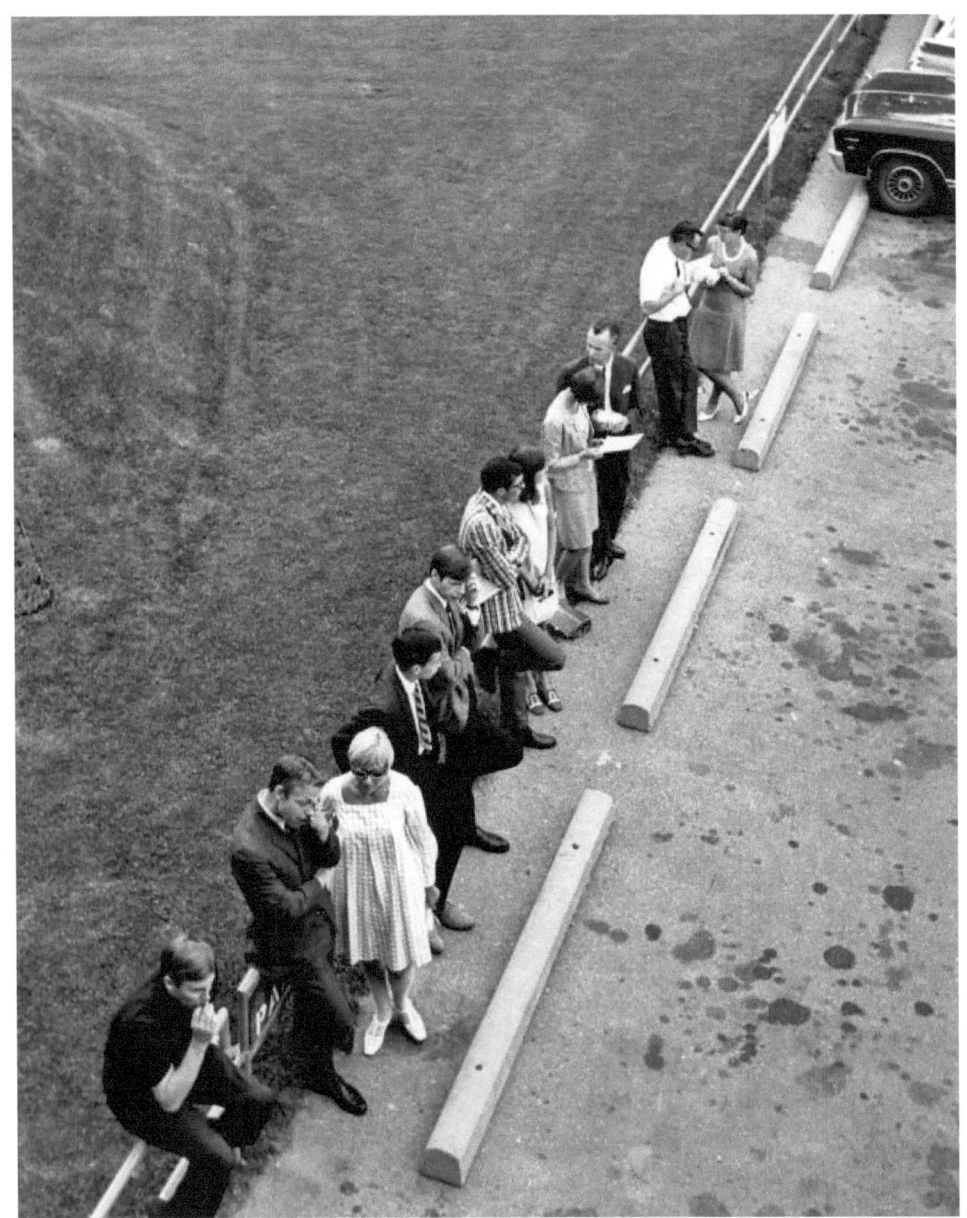

16

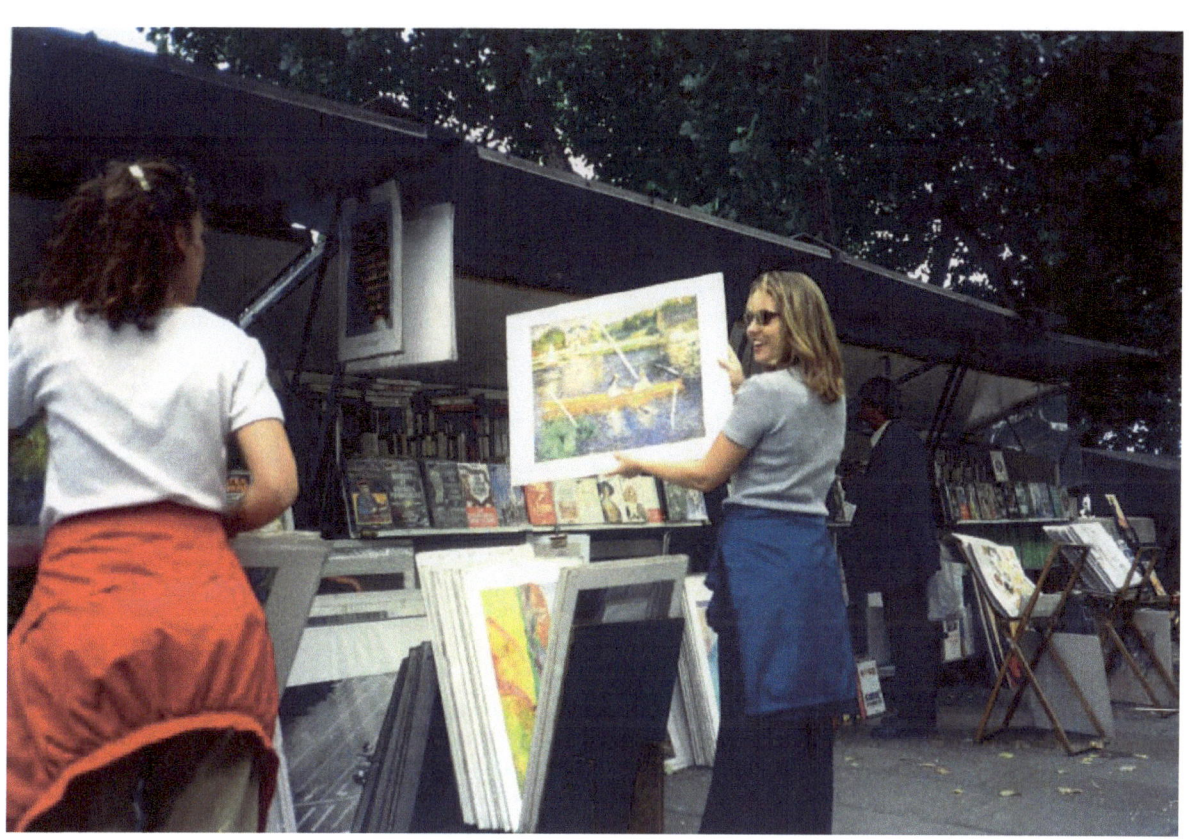

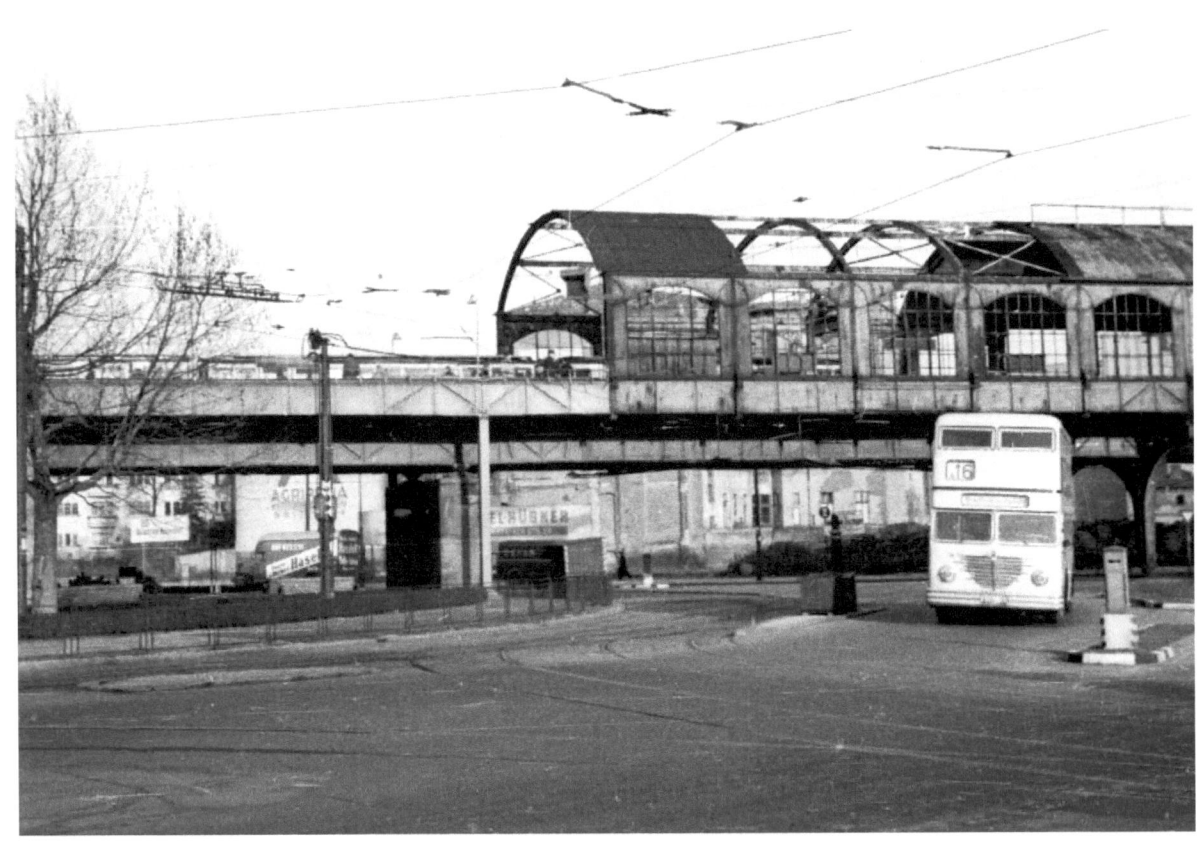

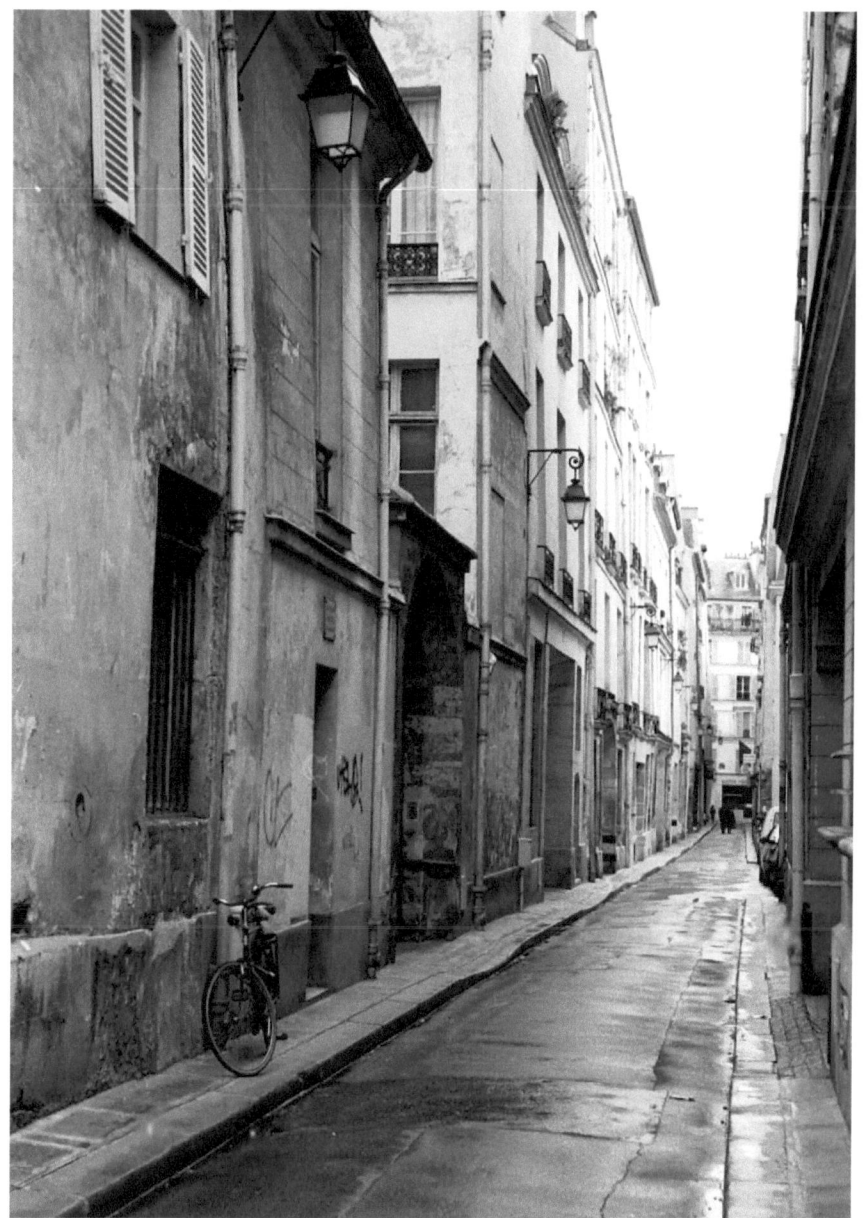

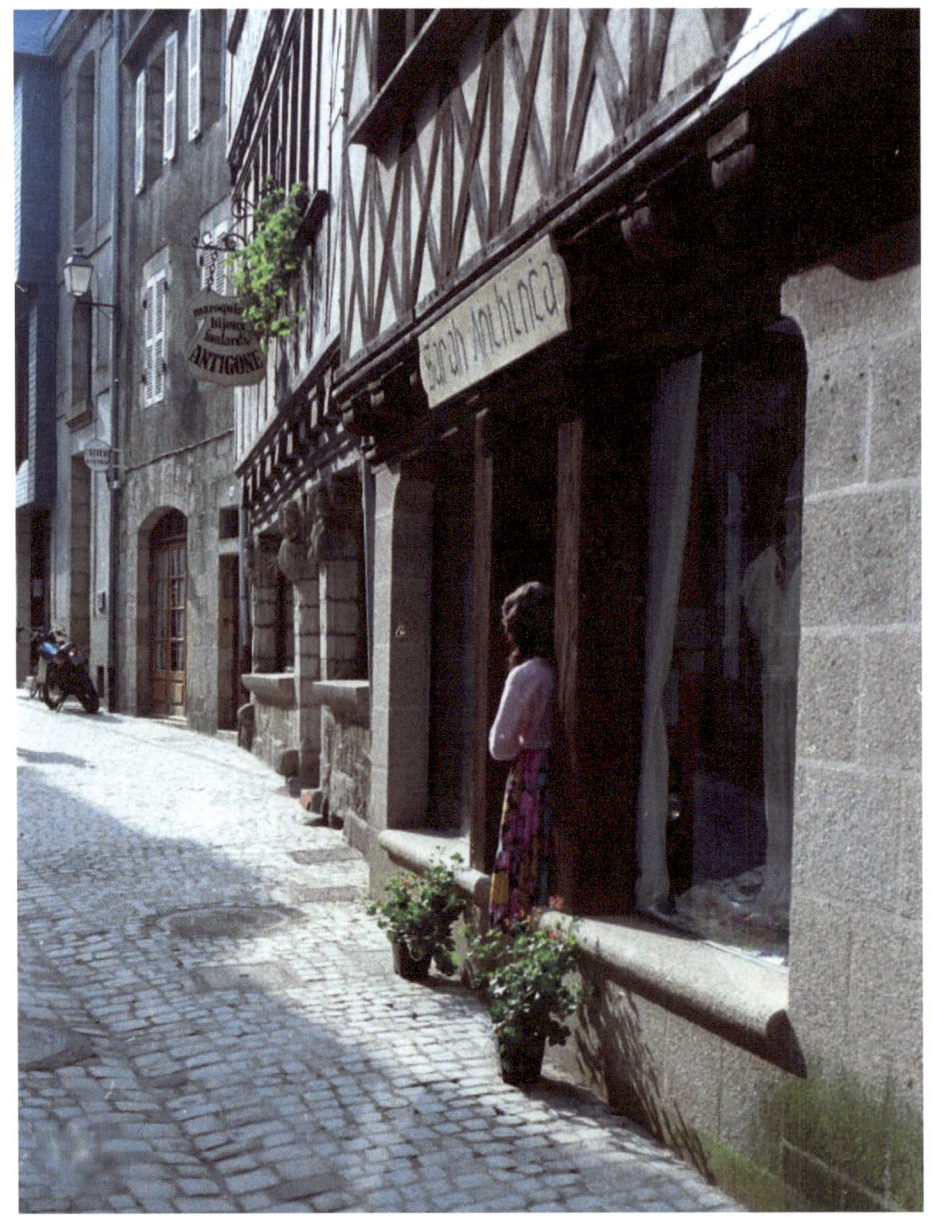

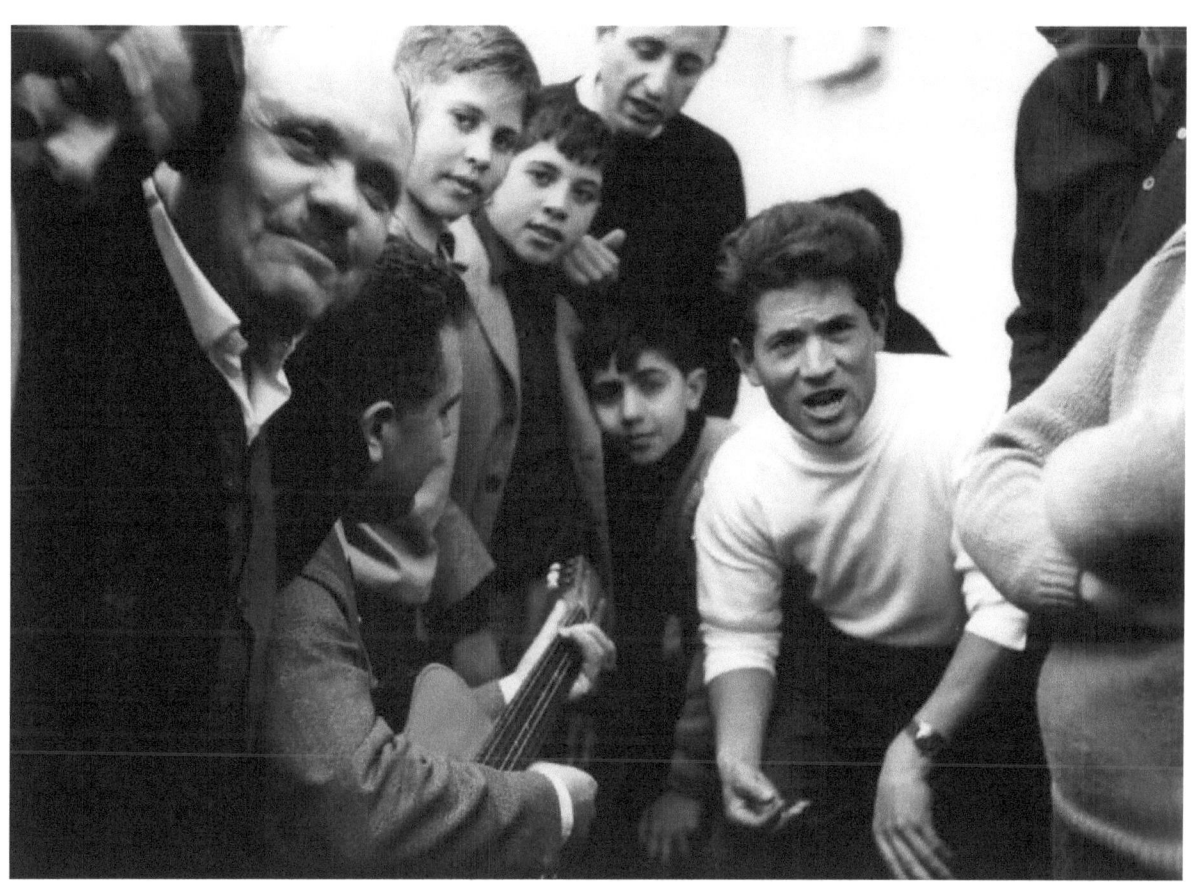

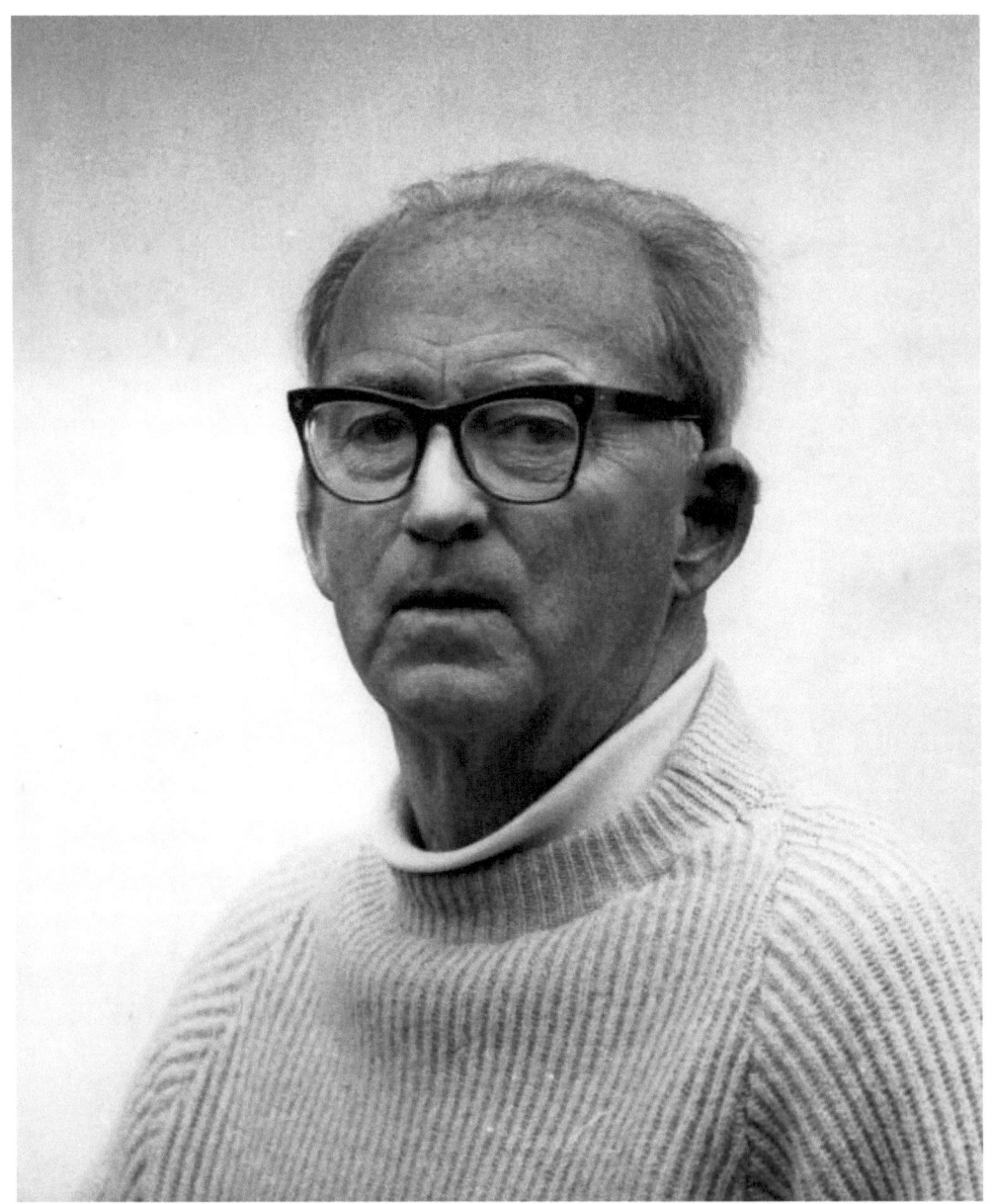

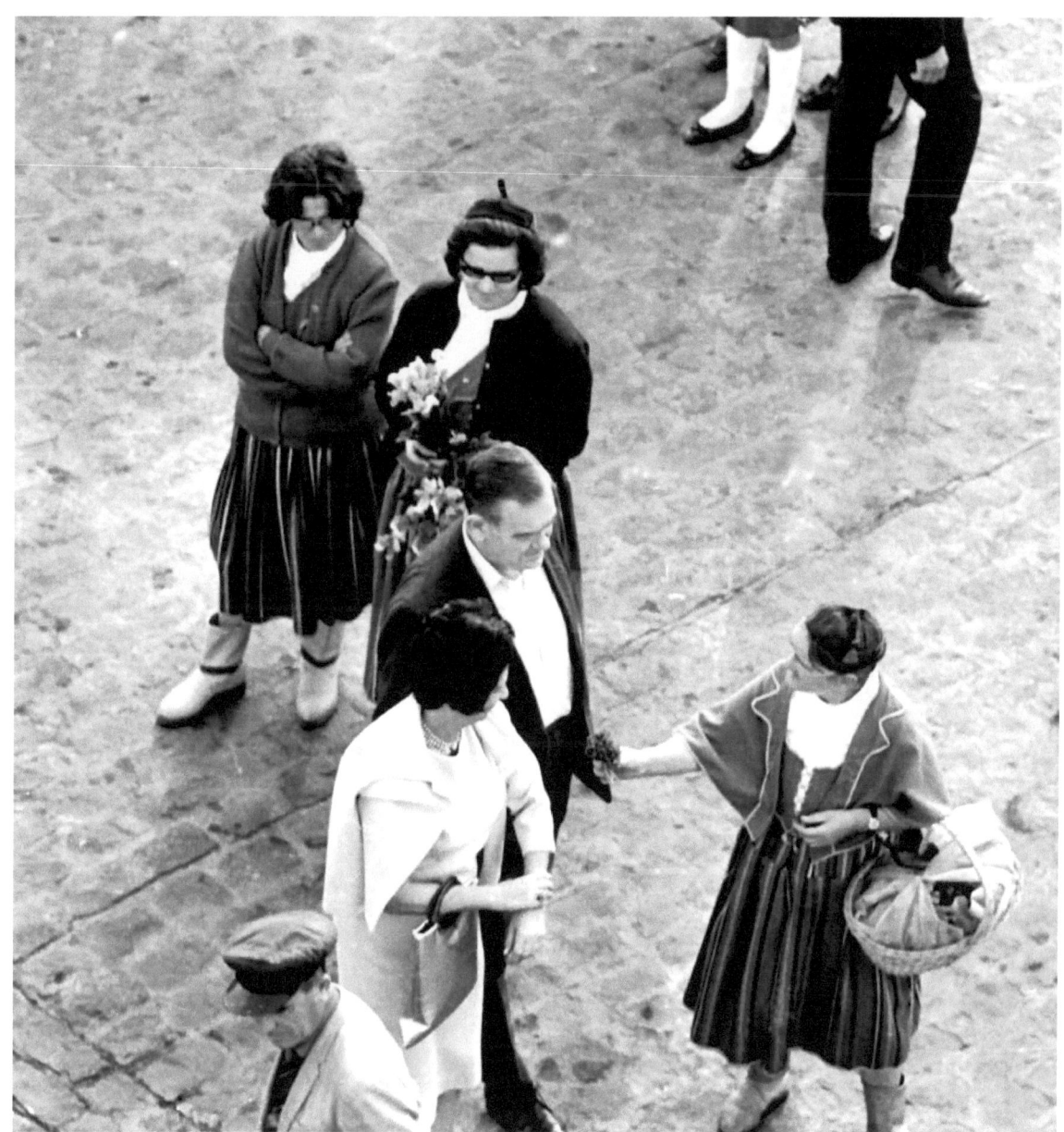

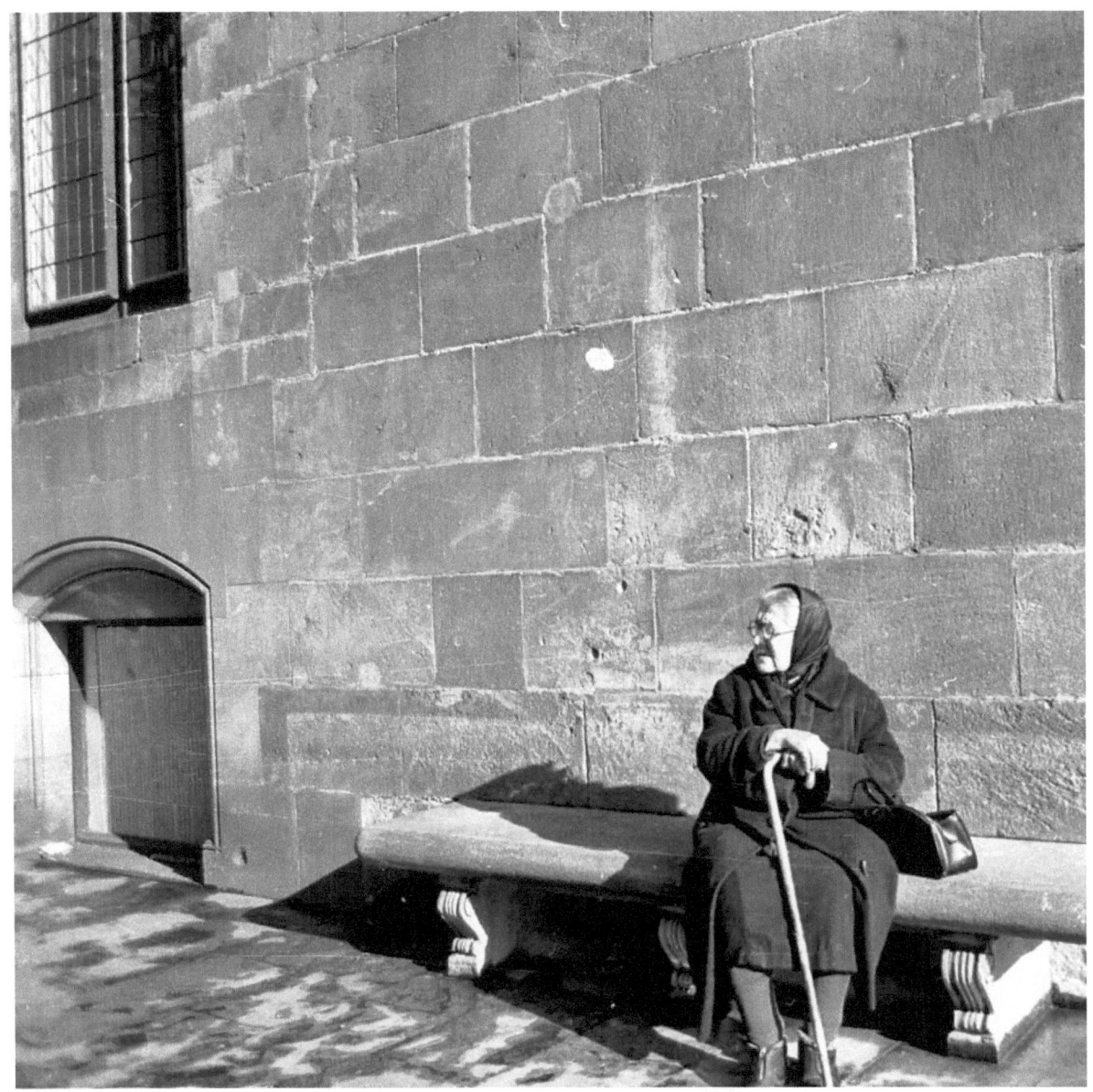

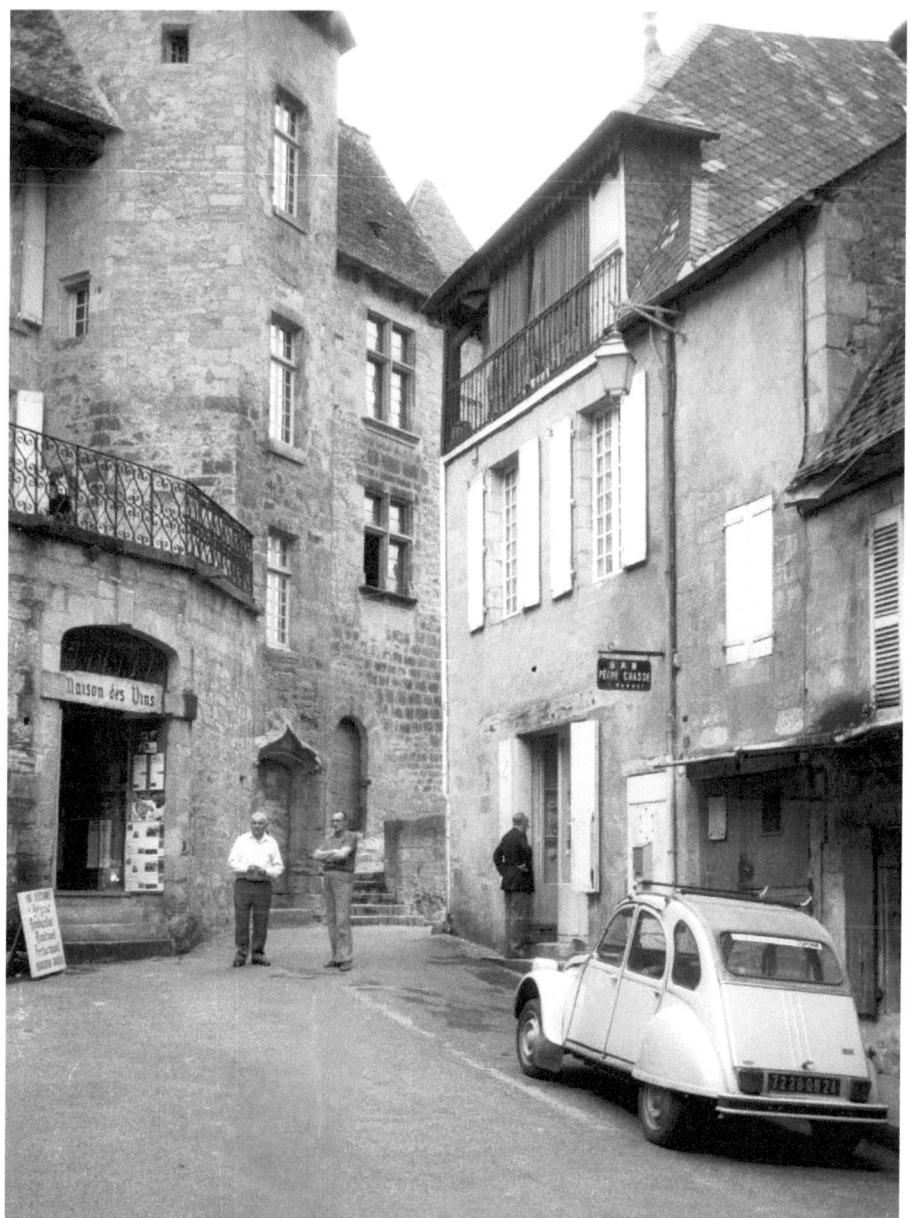

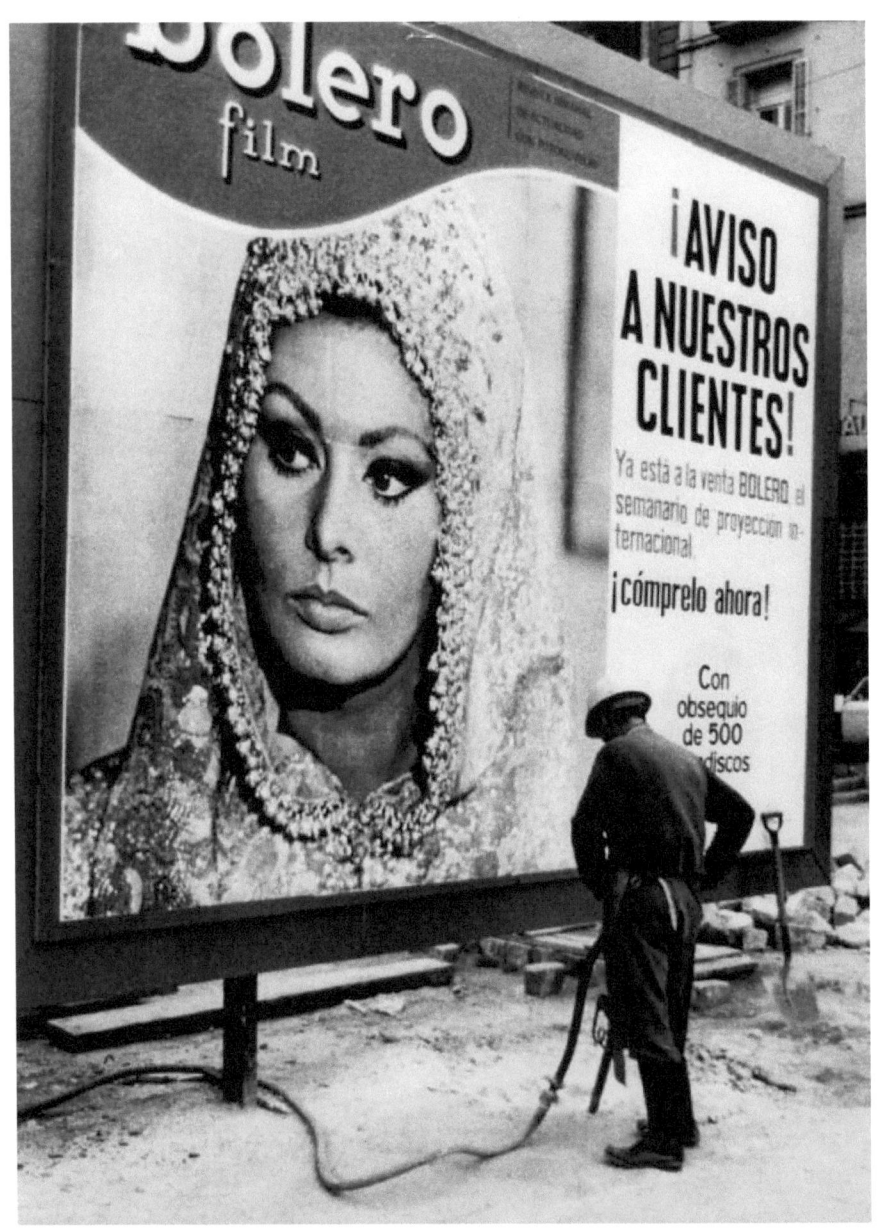

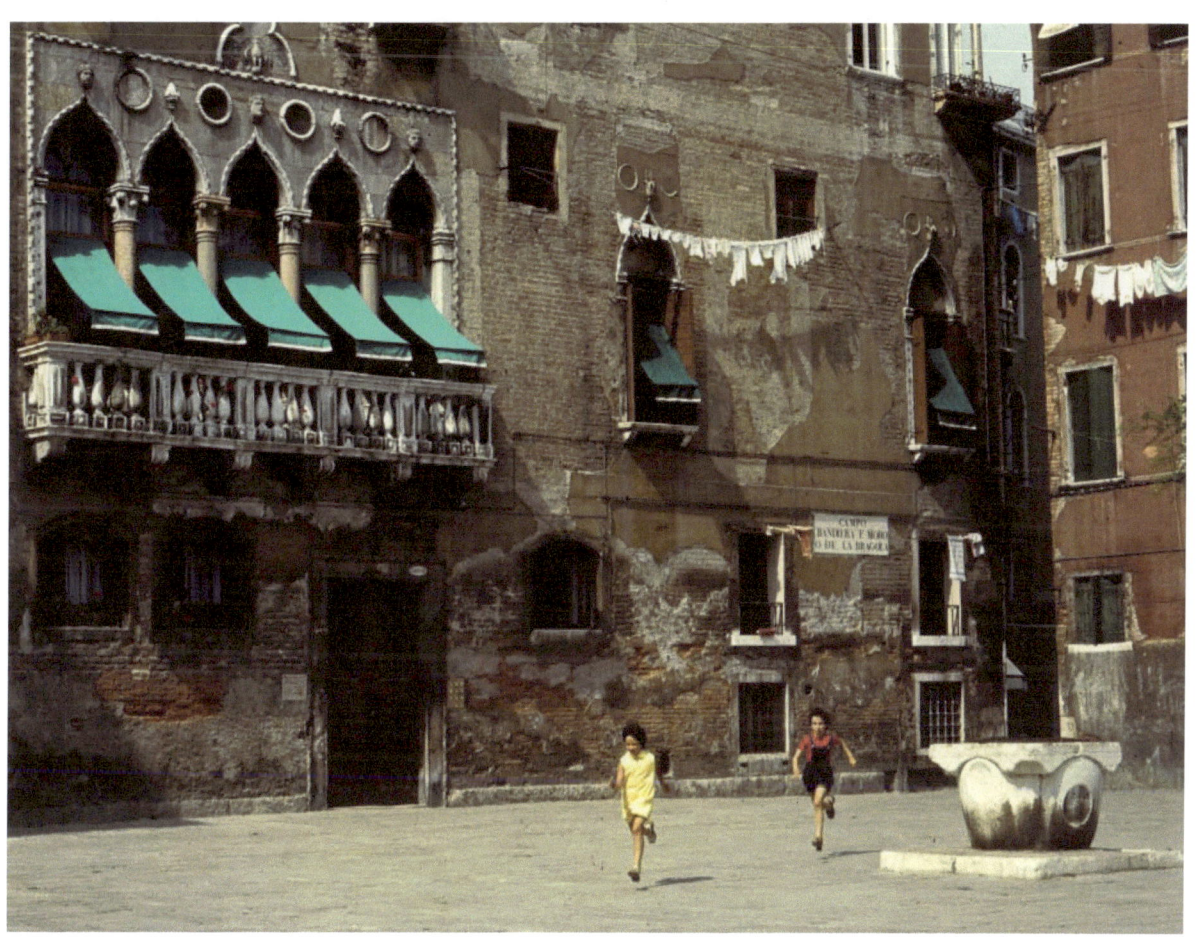

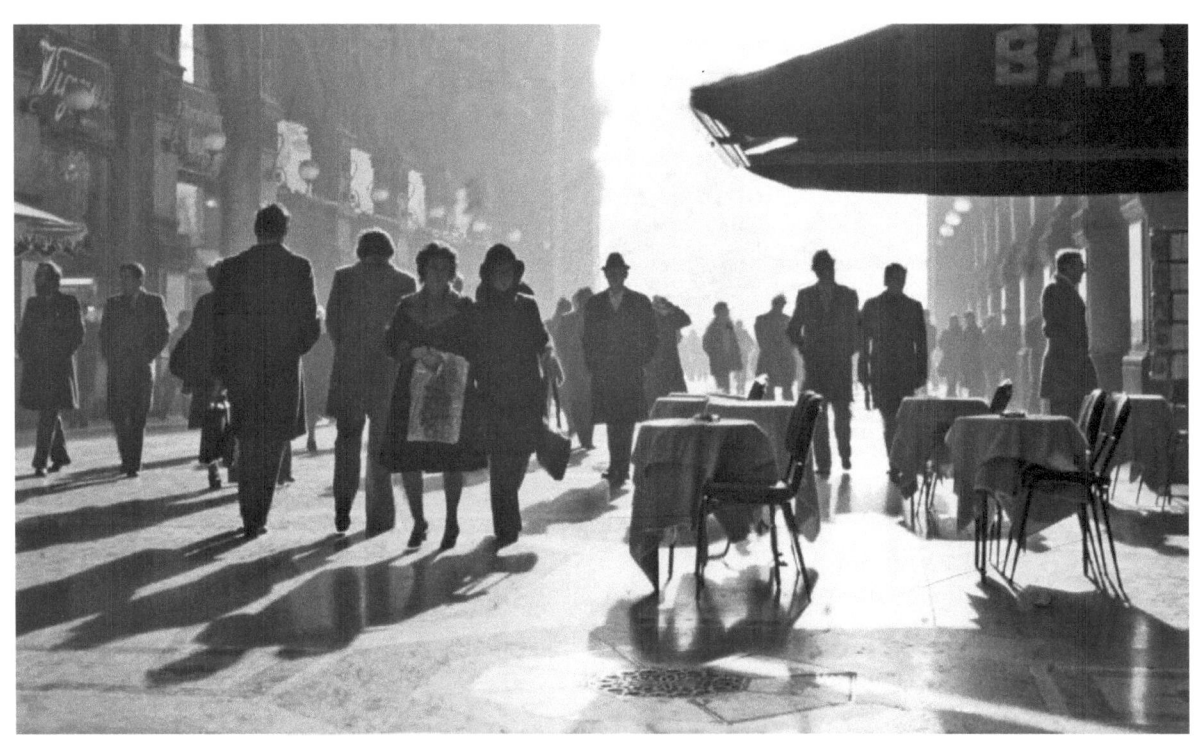

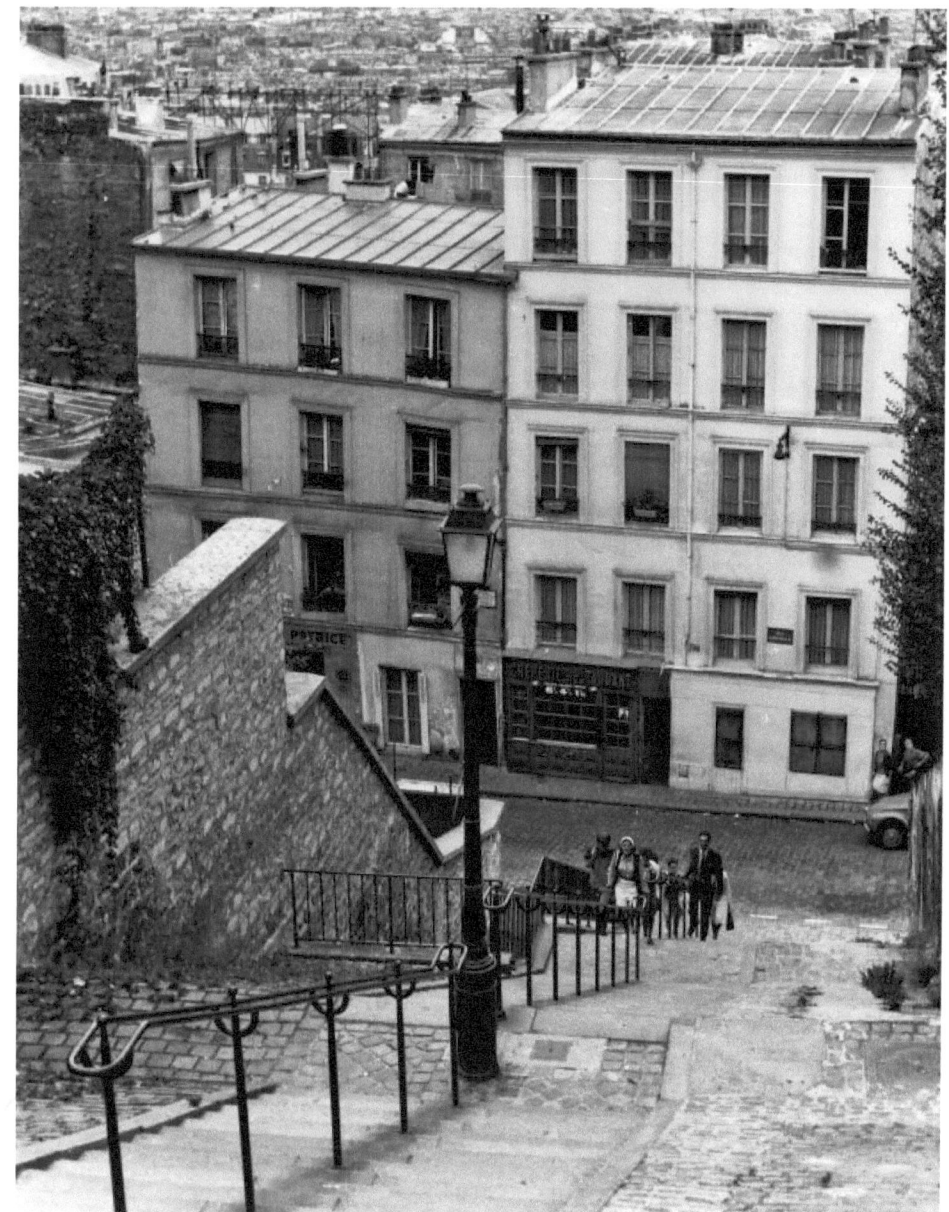

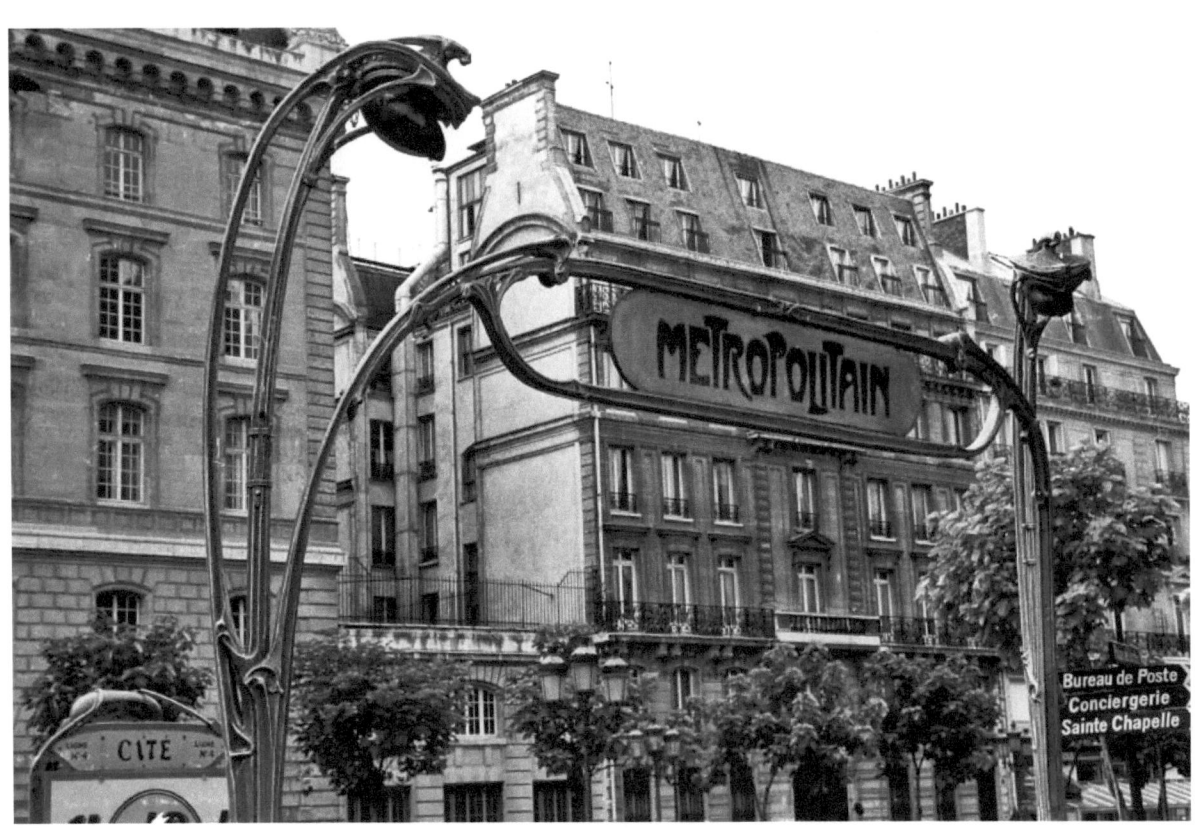

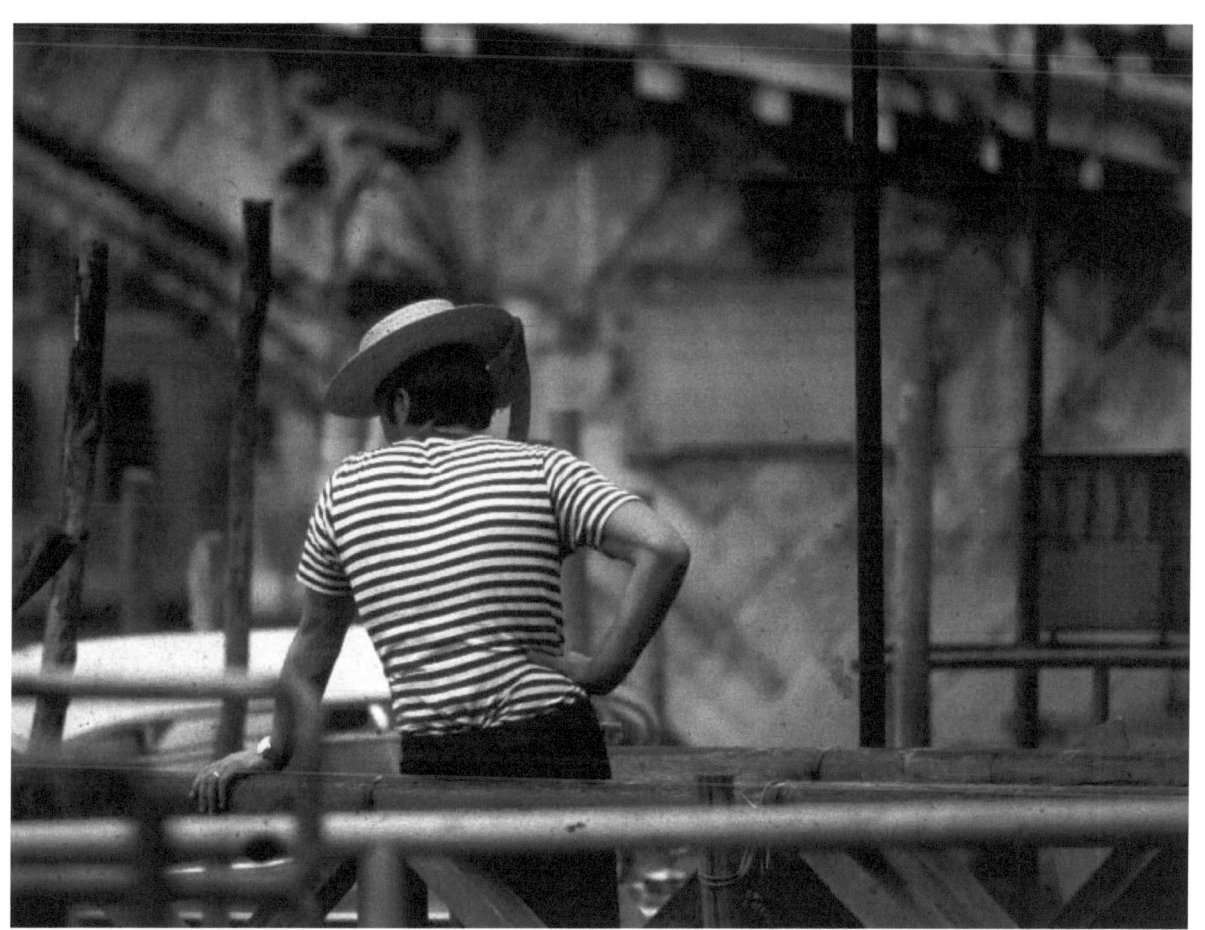

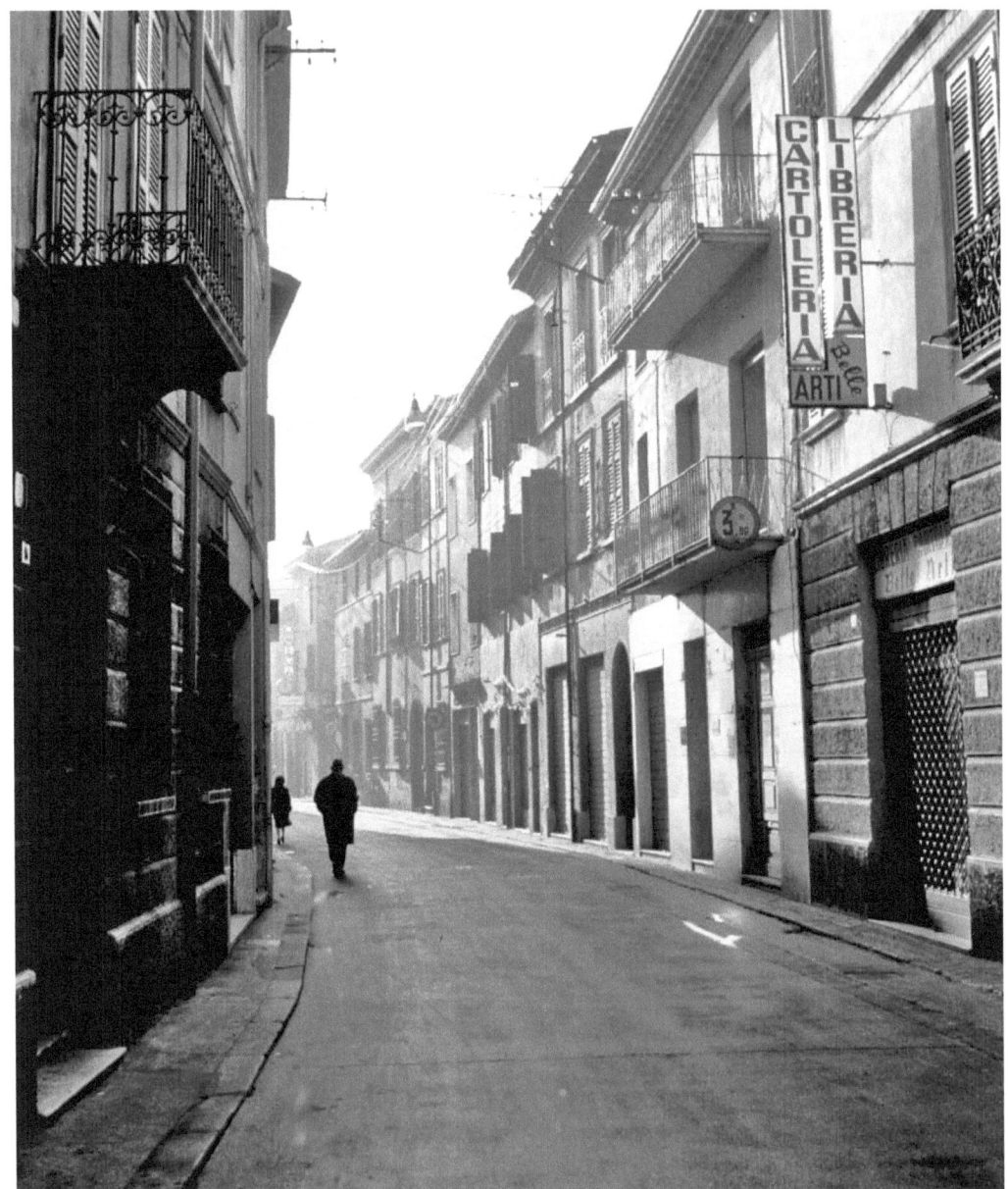

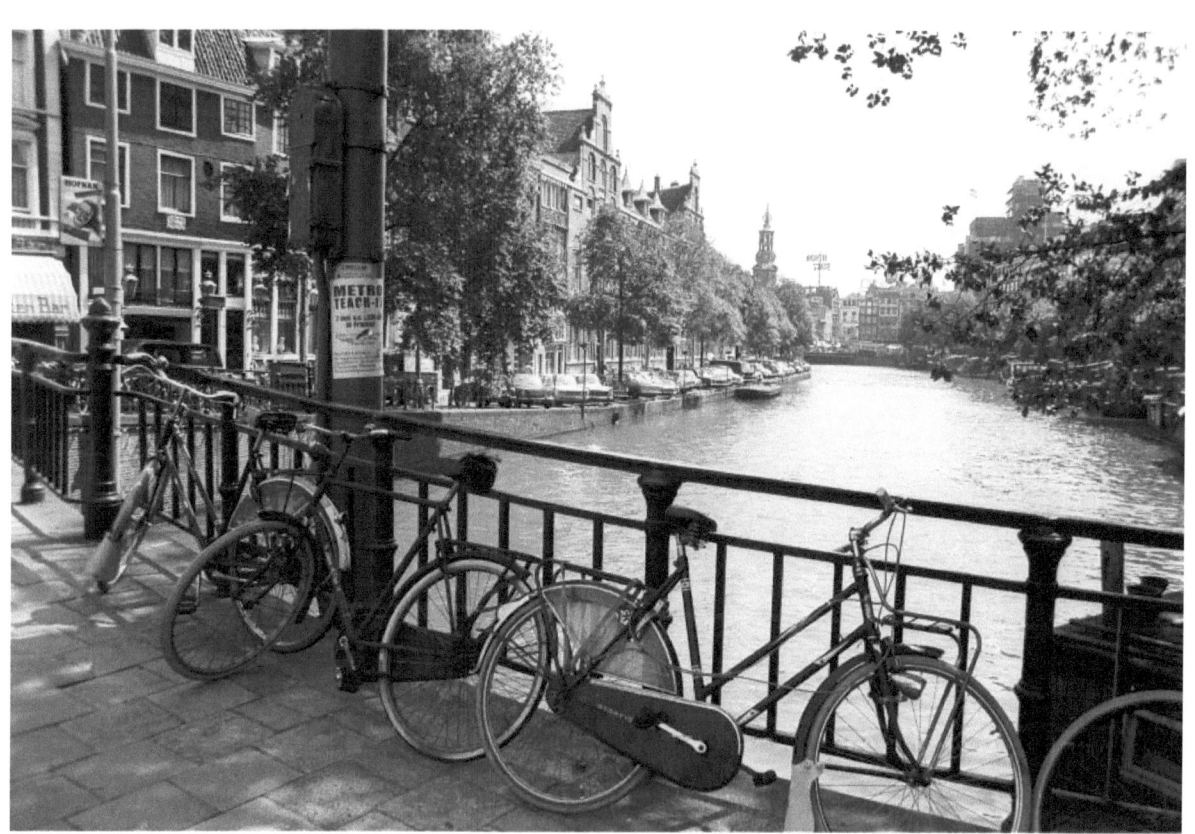

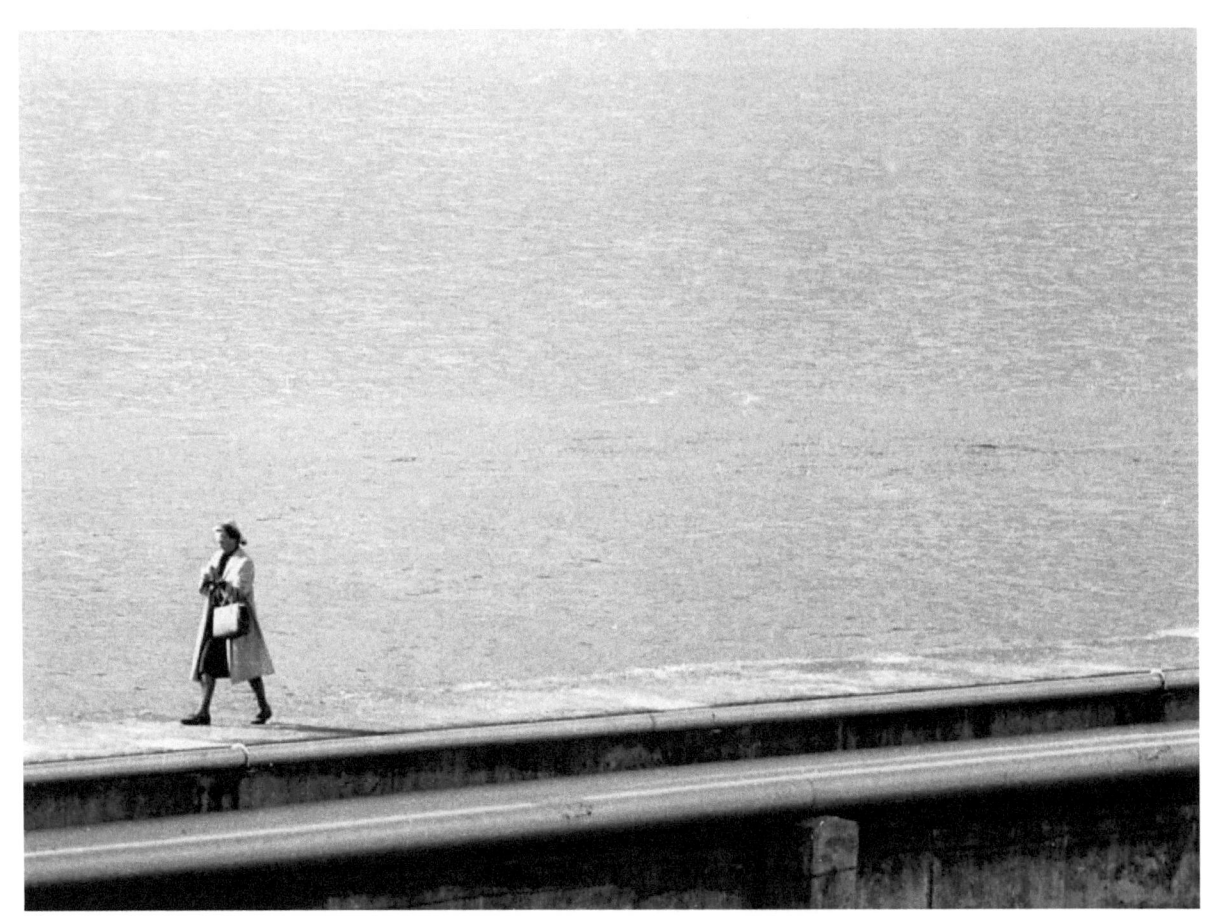

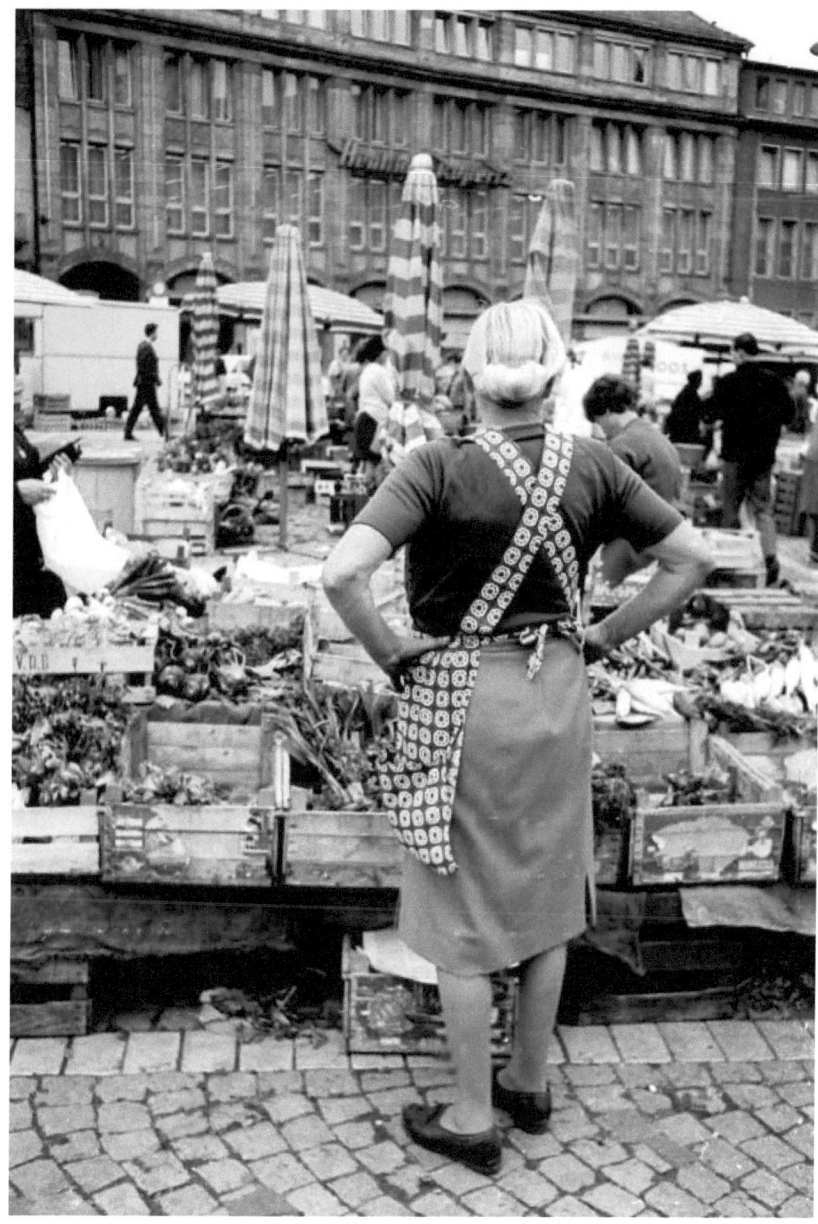

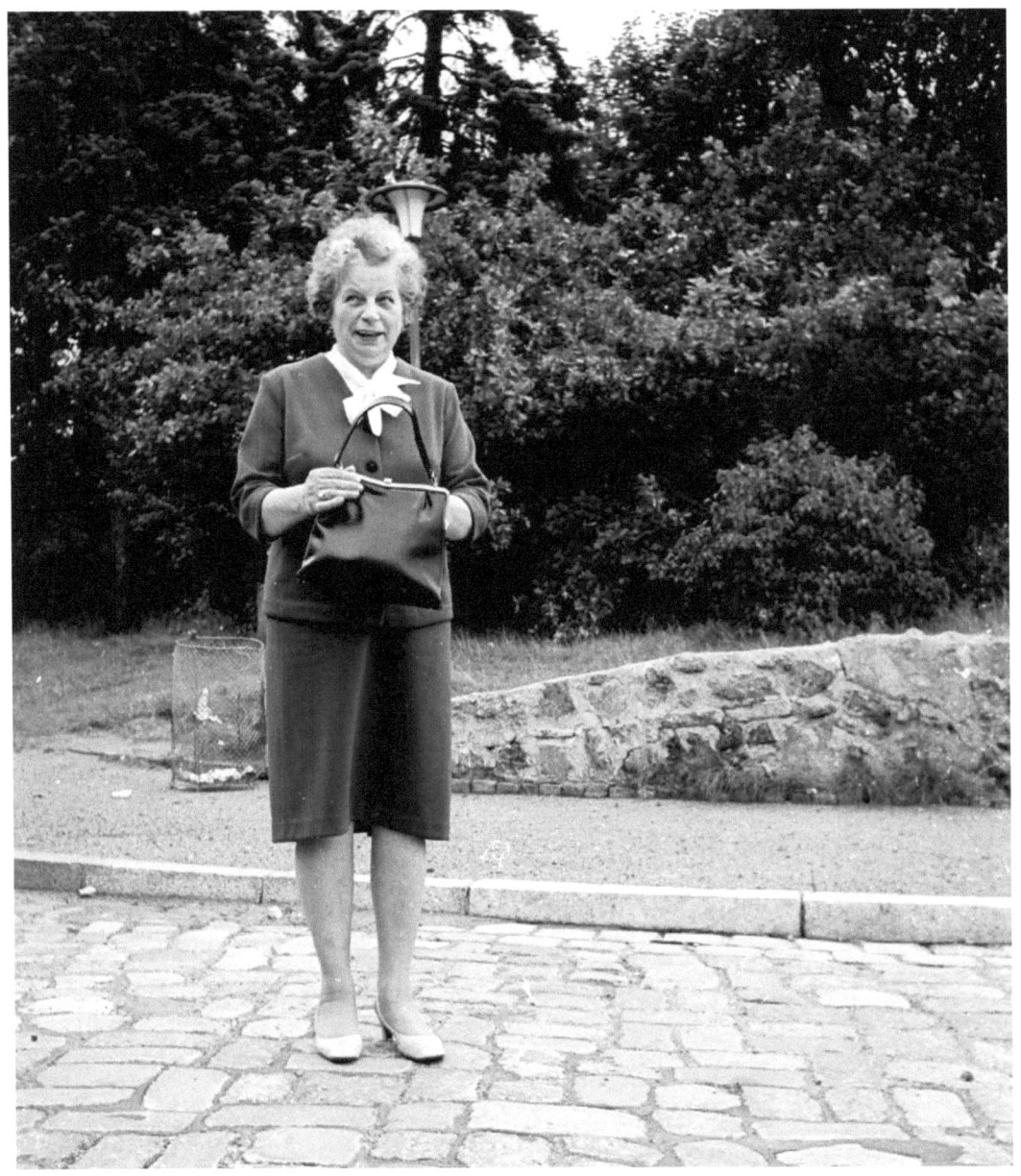

36

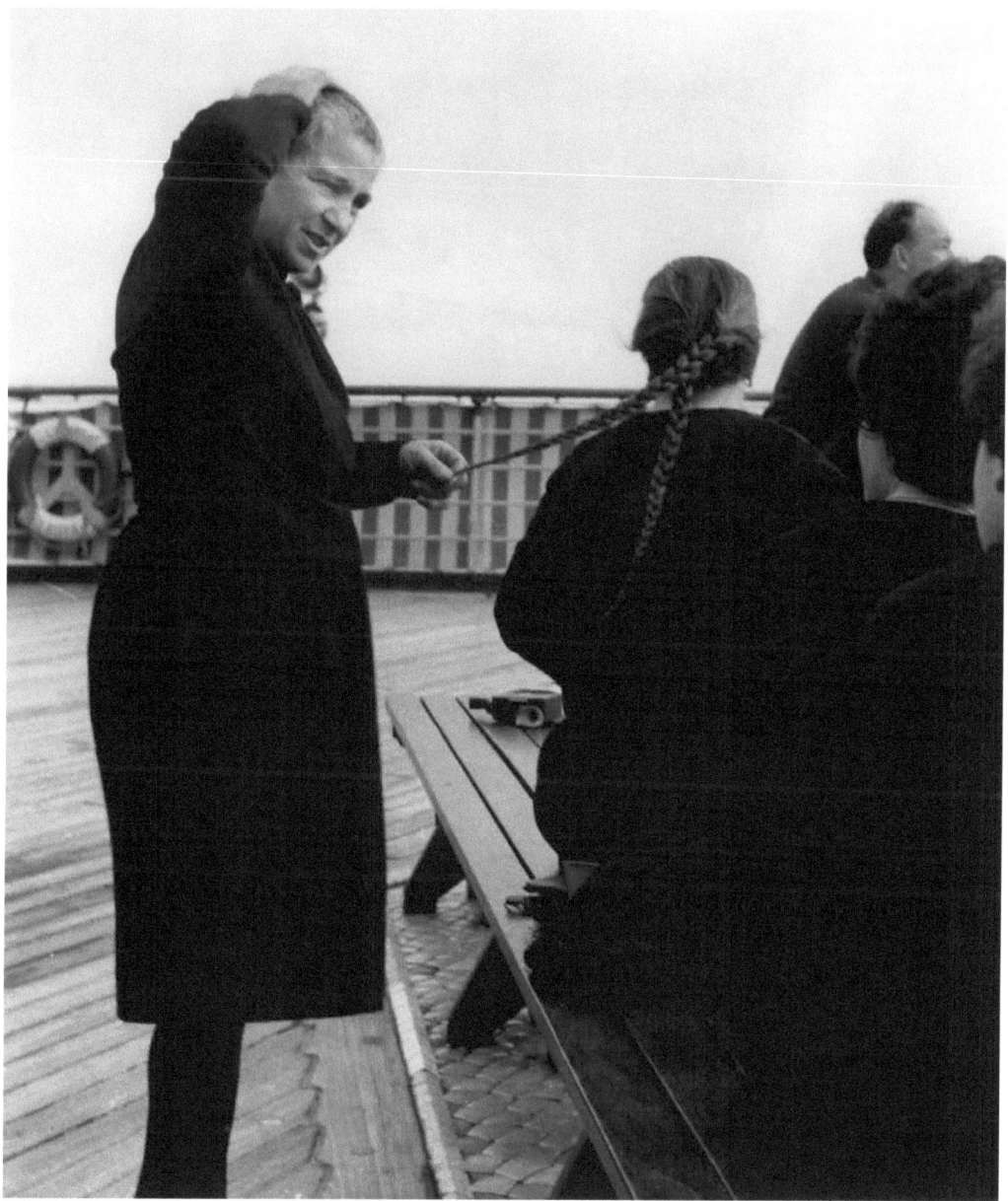

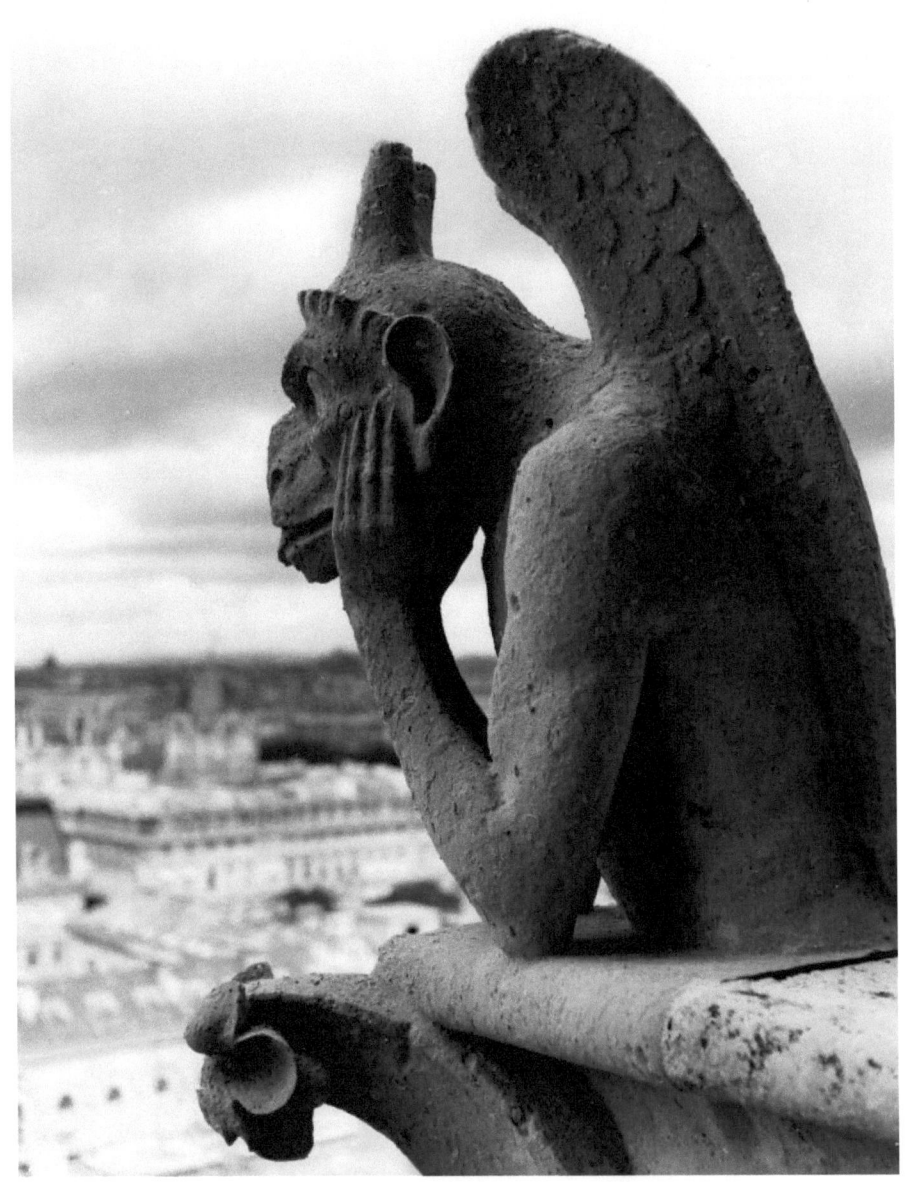

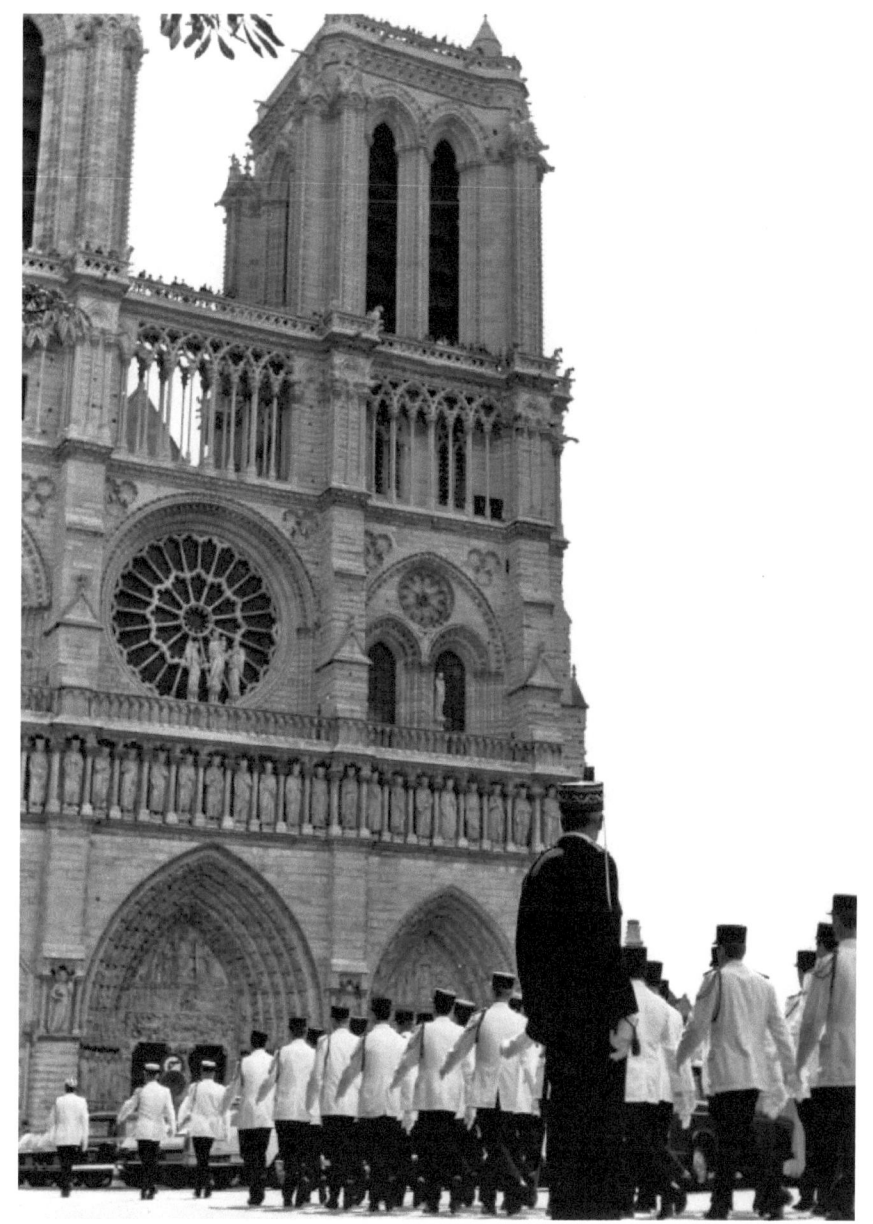

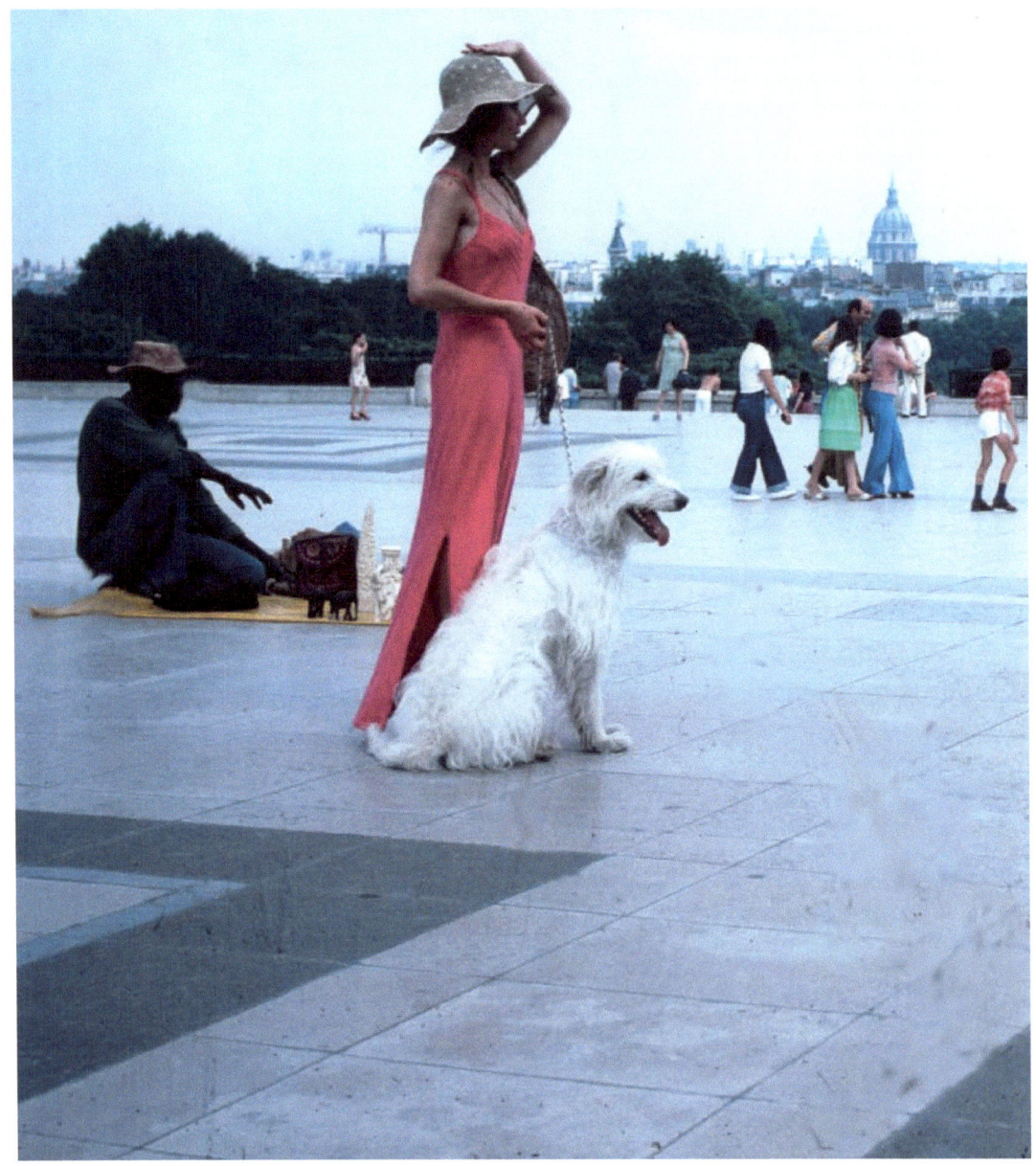

40

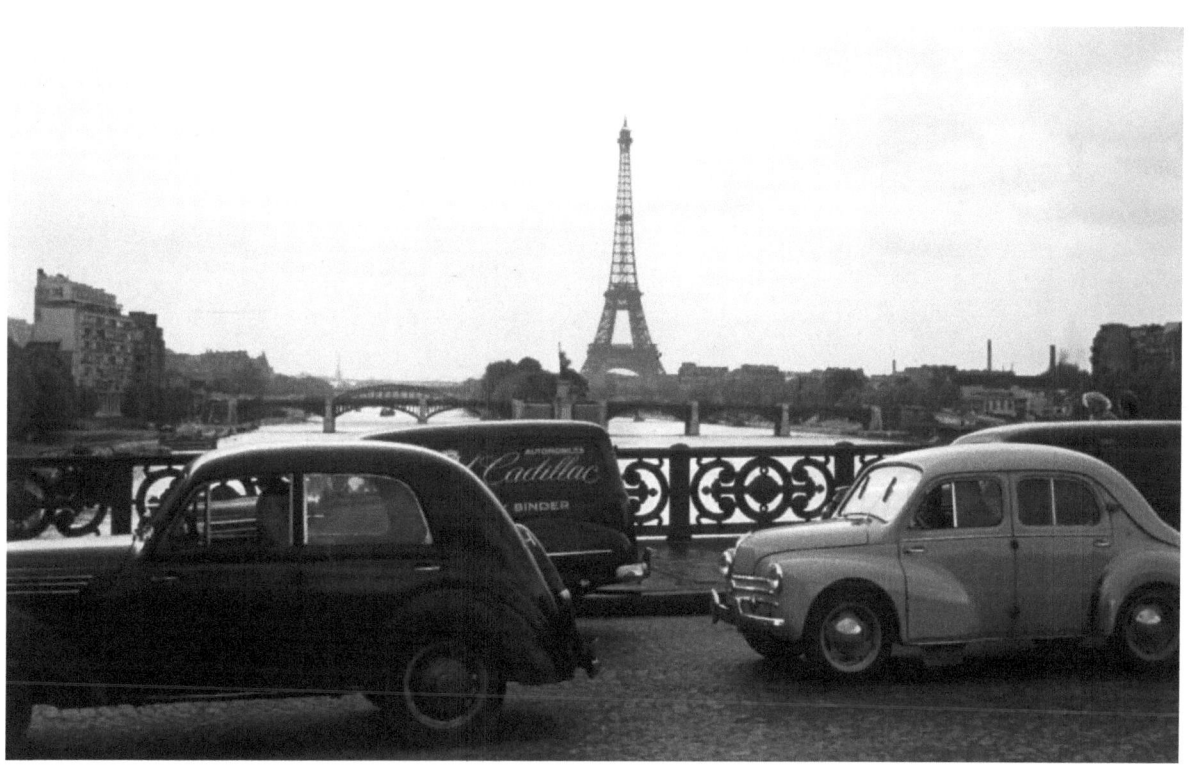

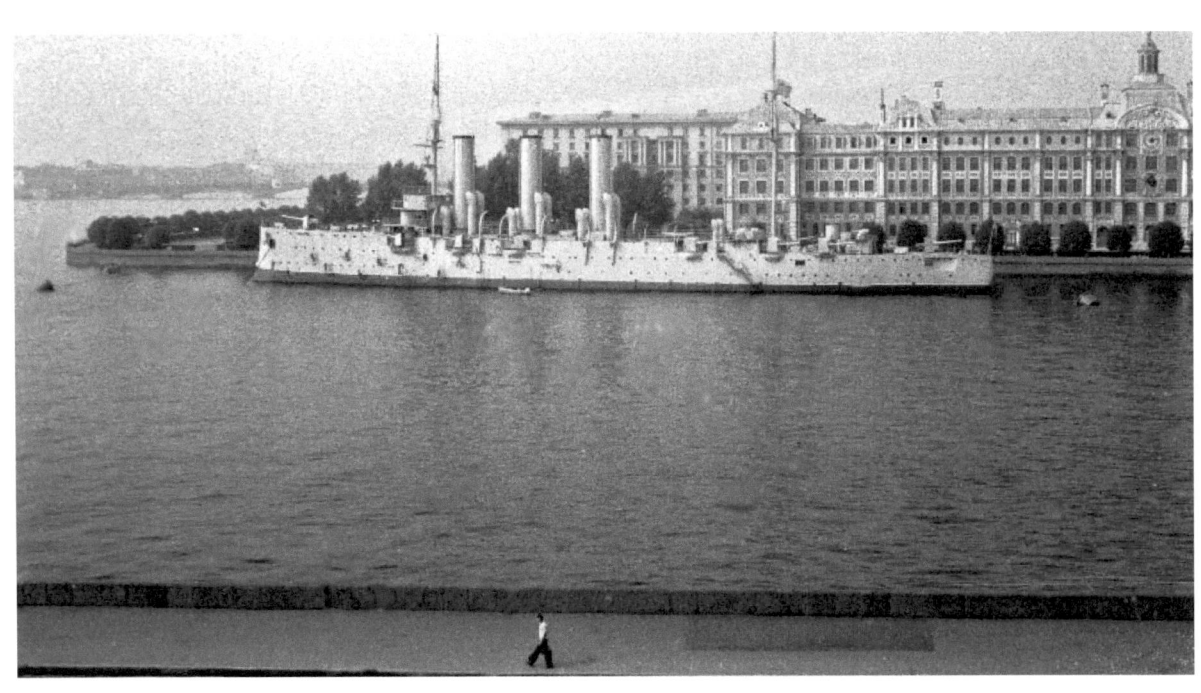

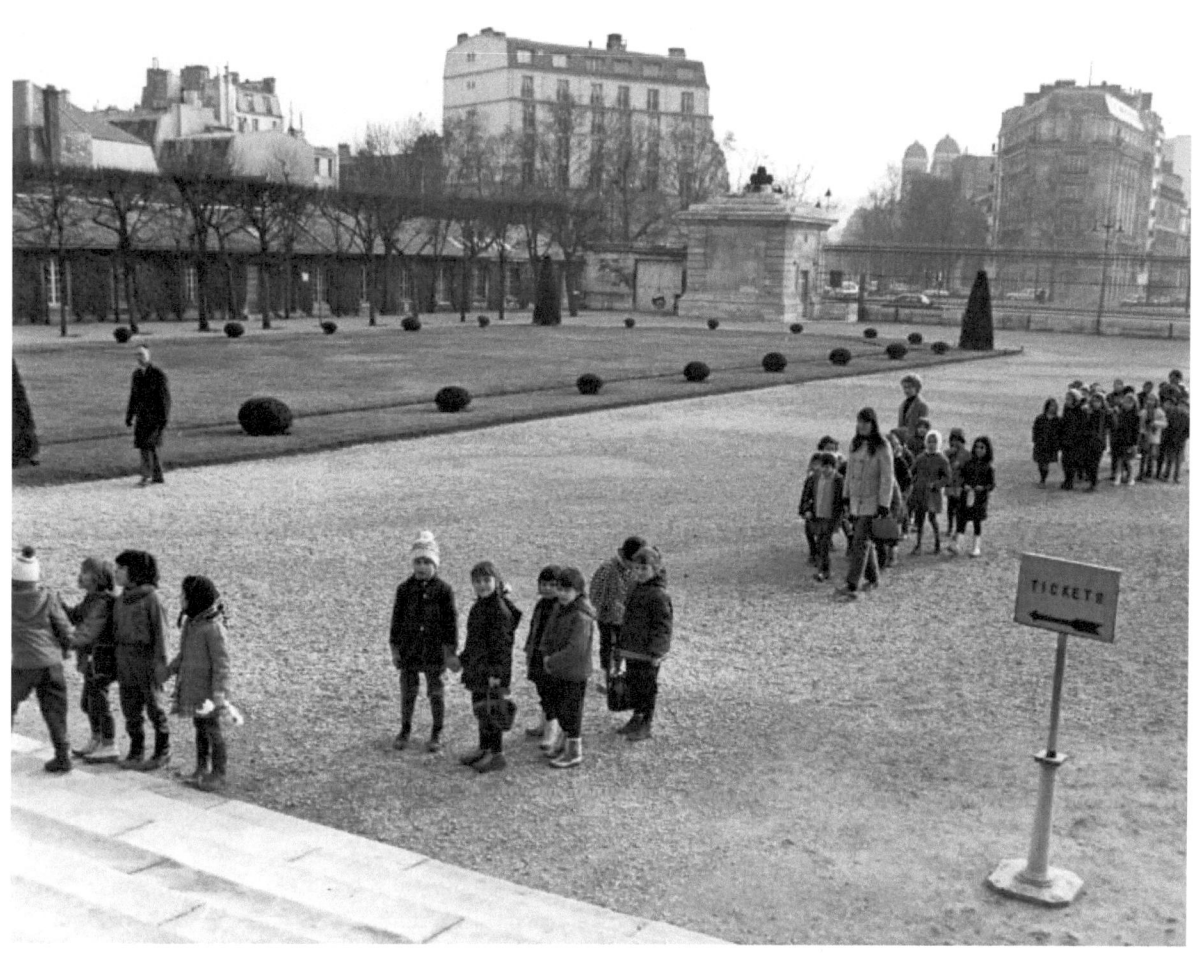

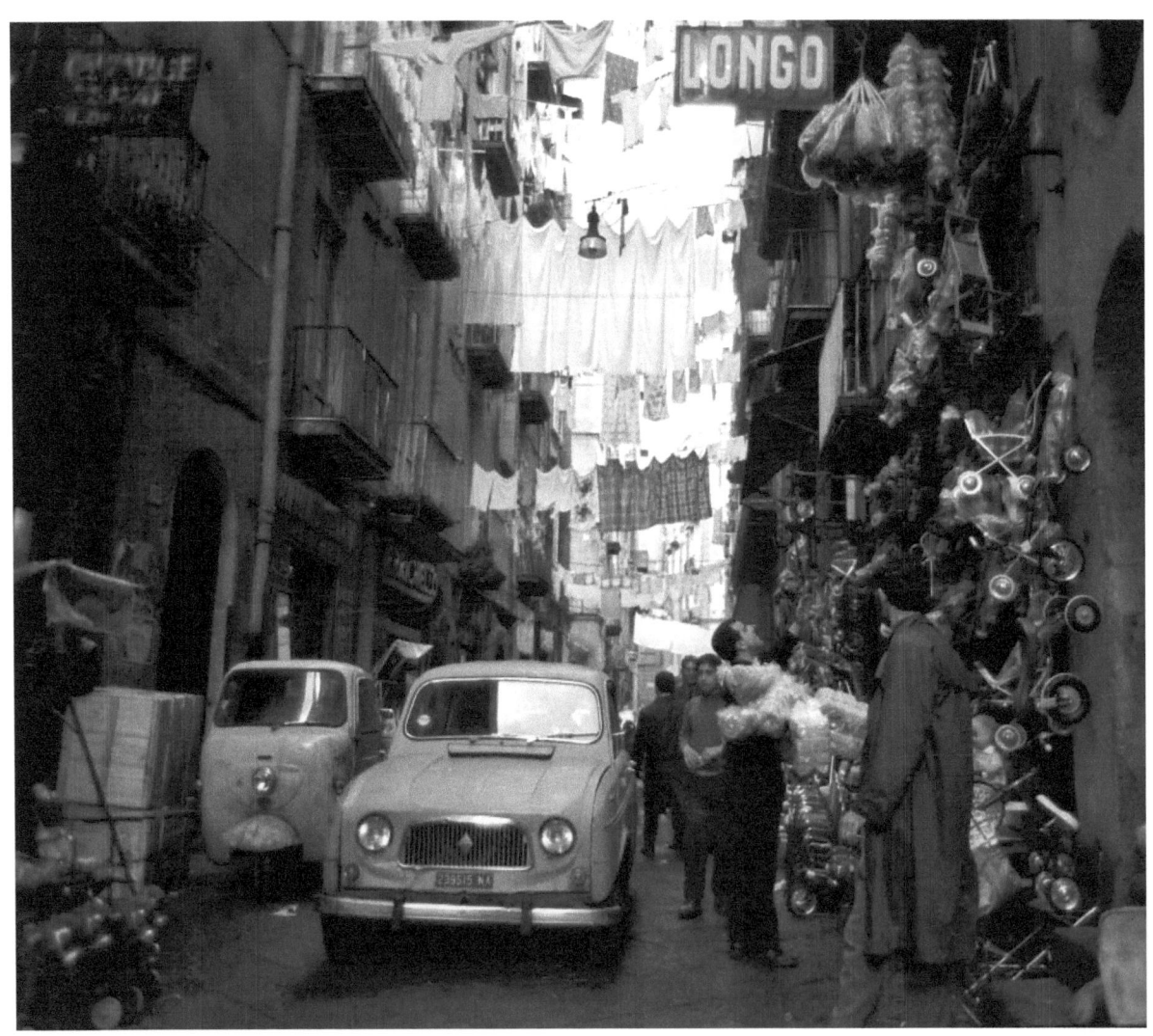

44

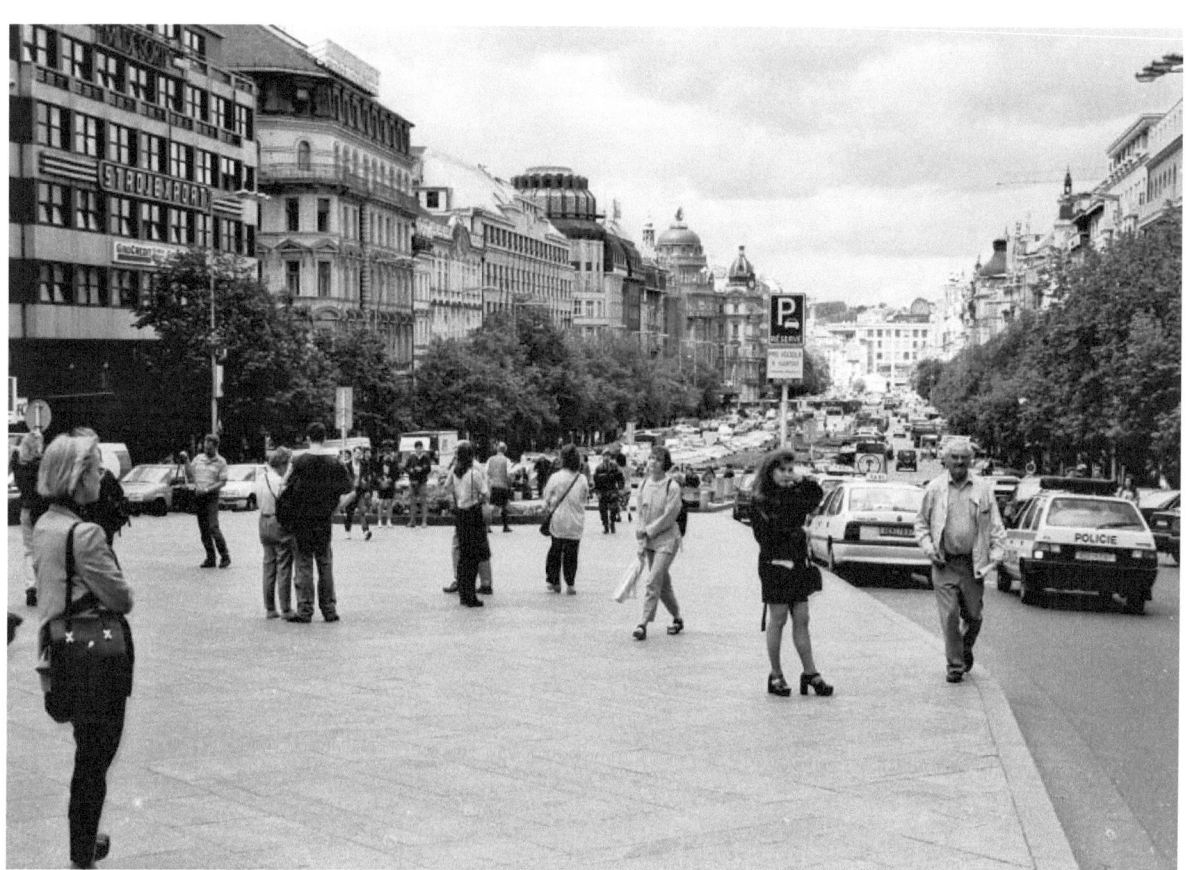

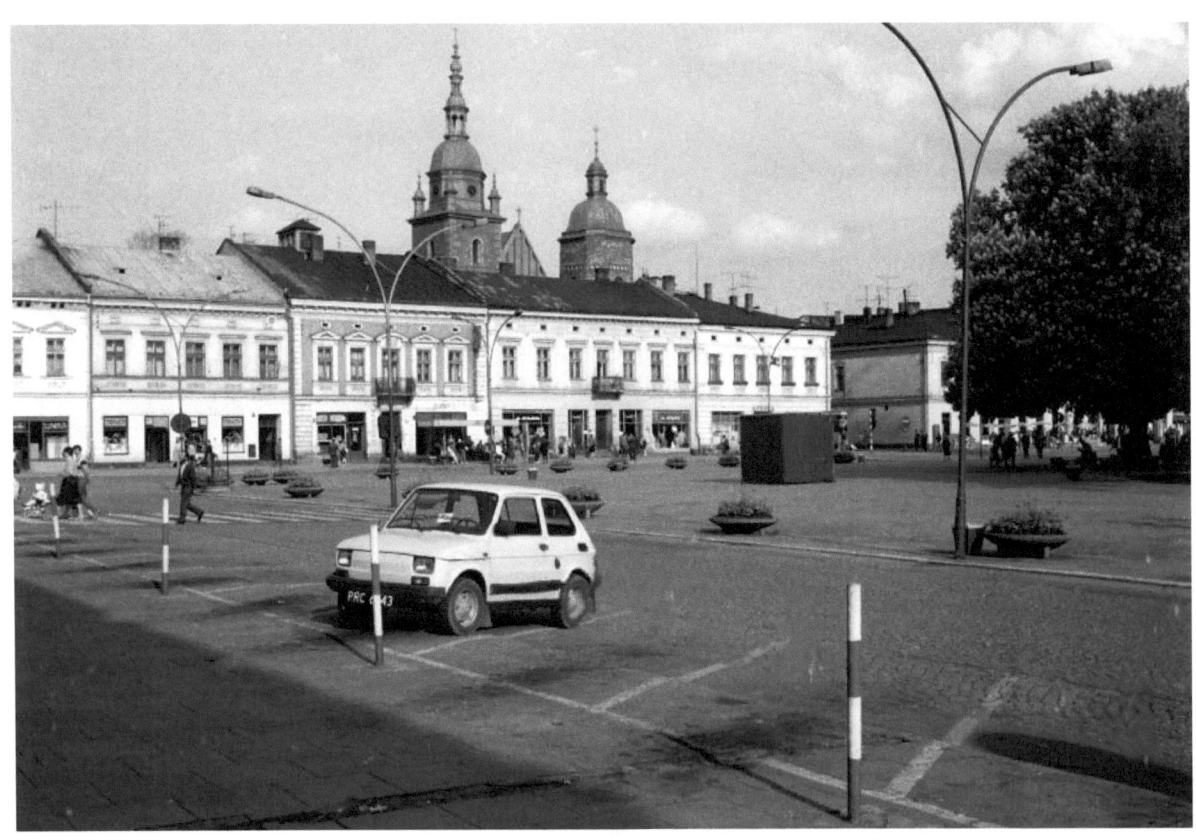

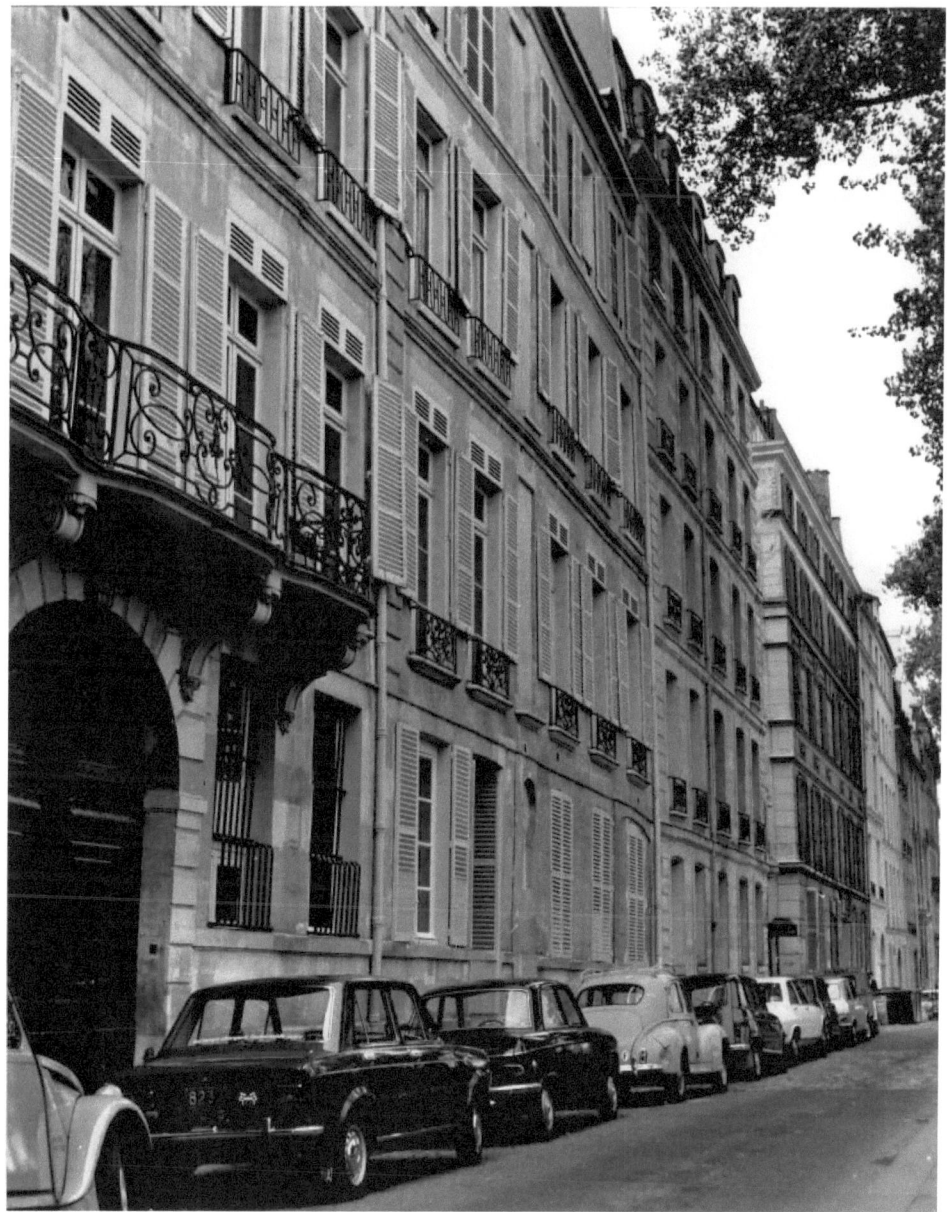

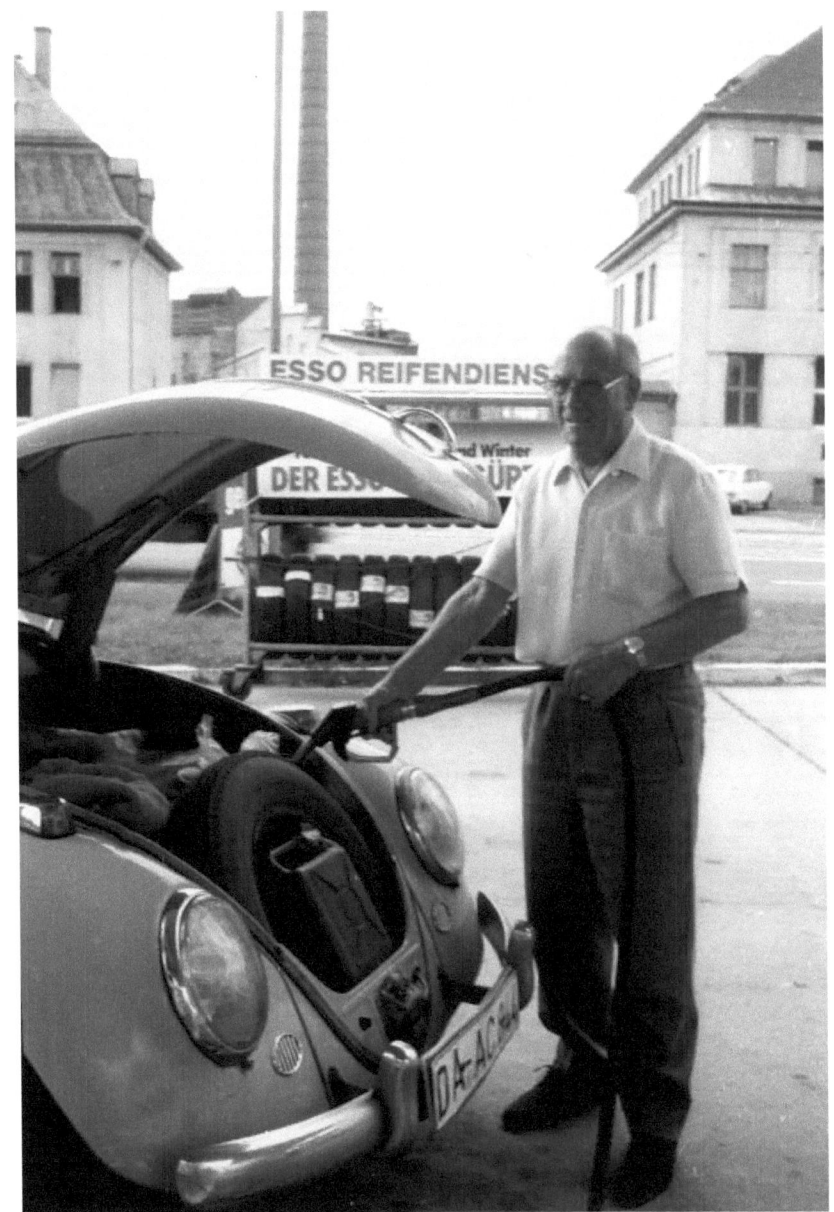

48

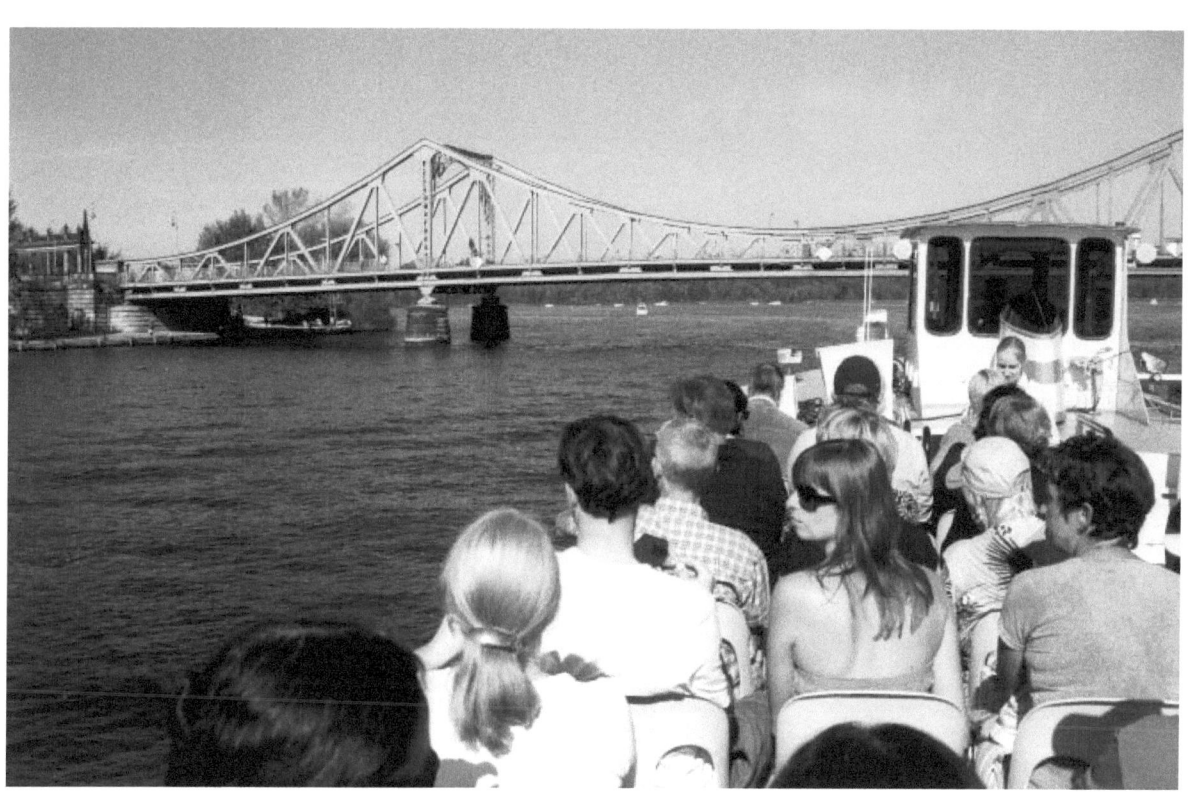

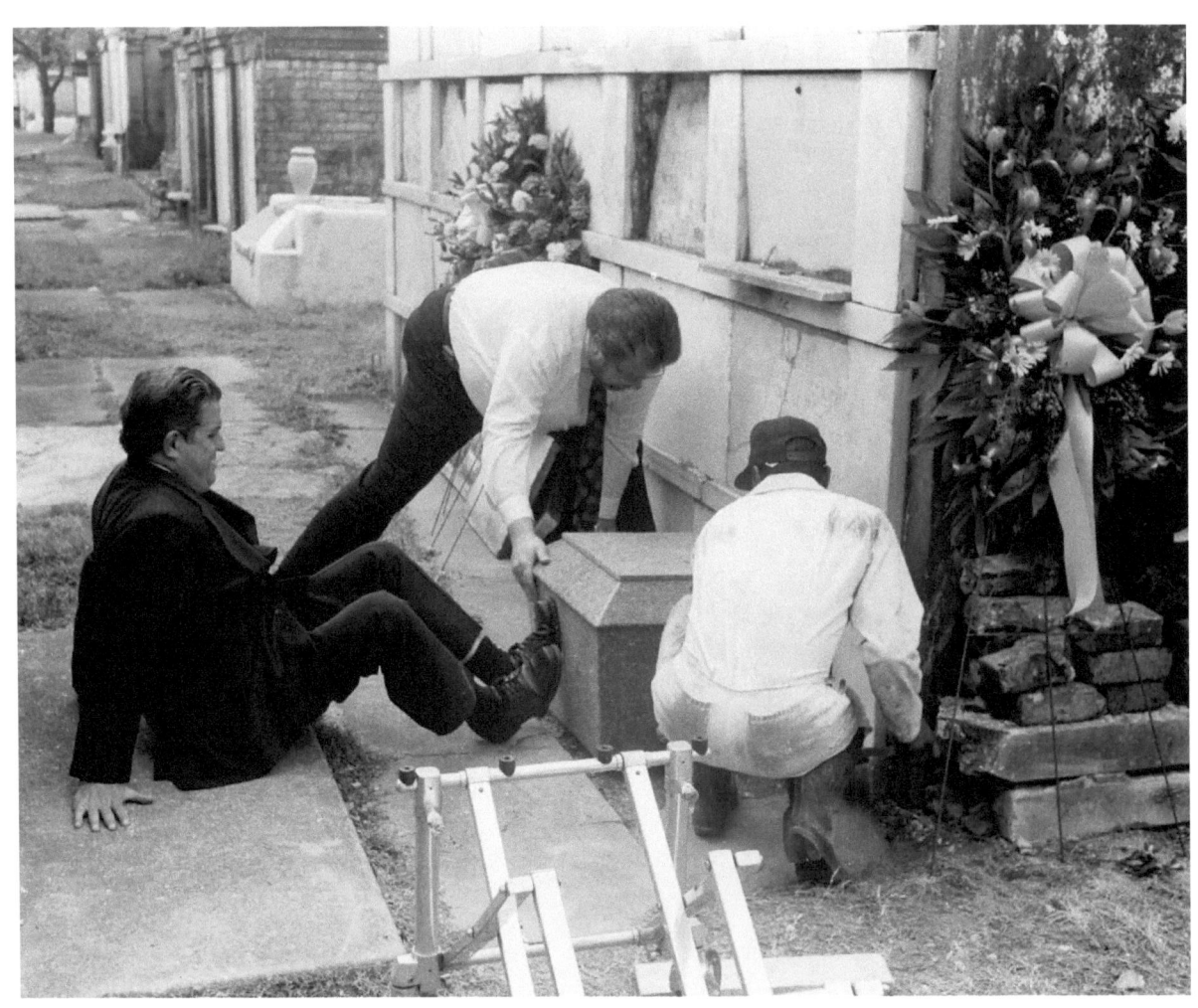

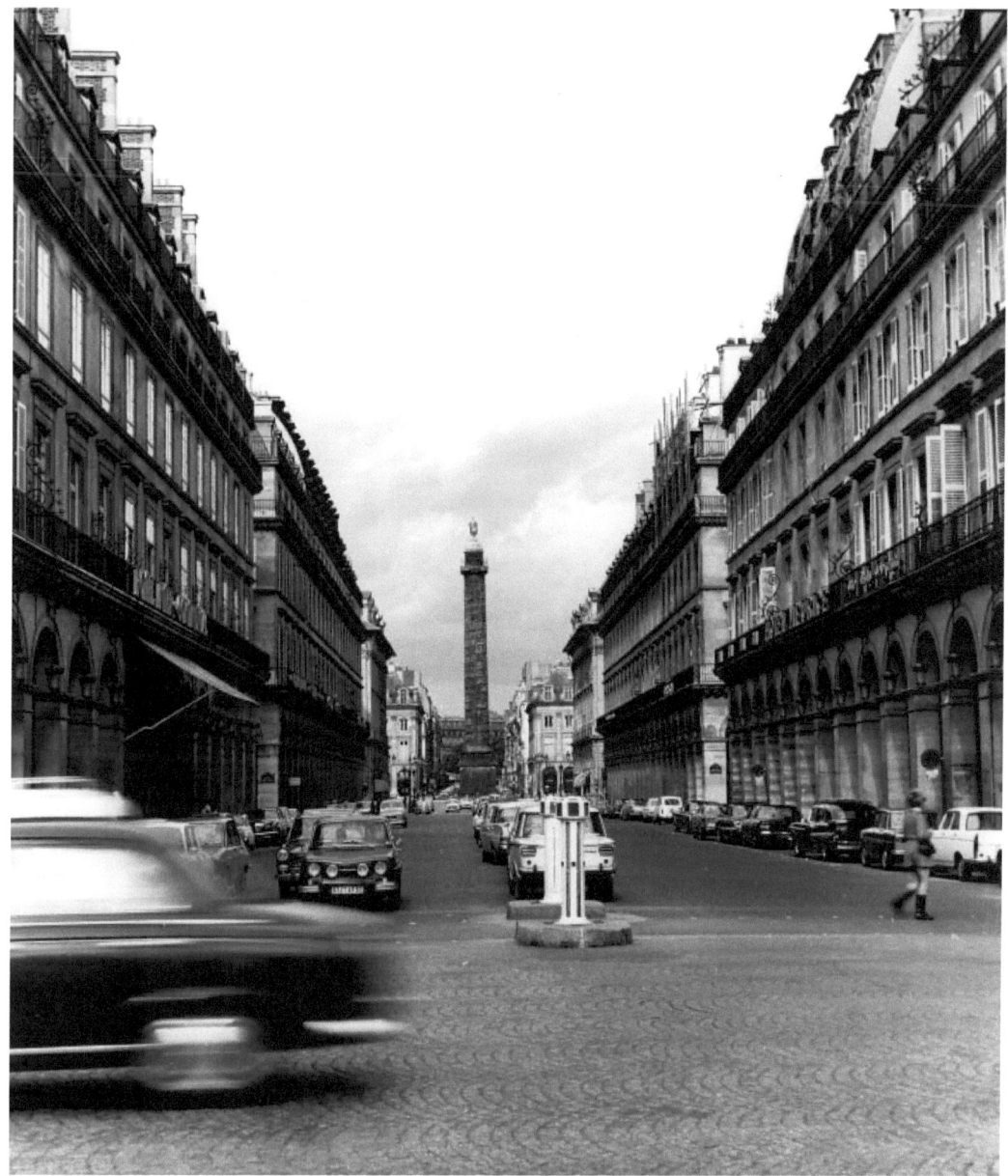

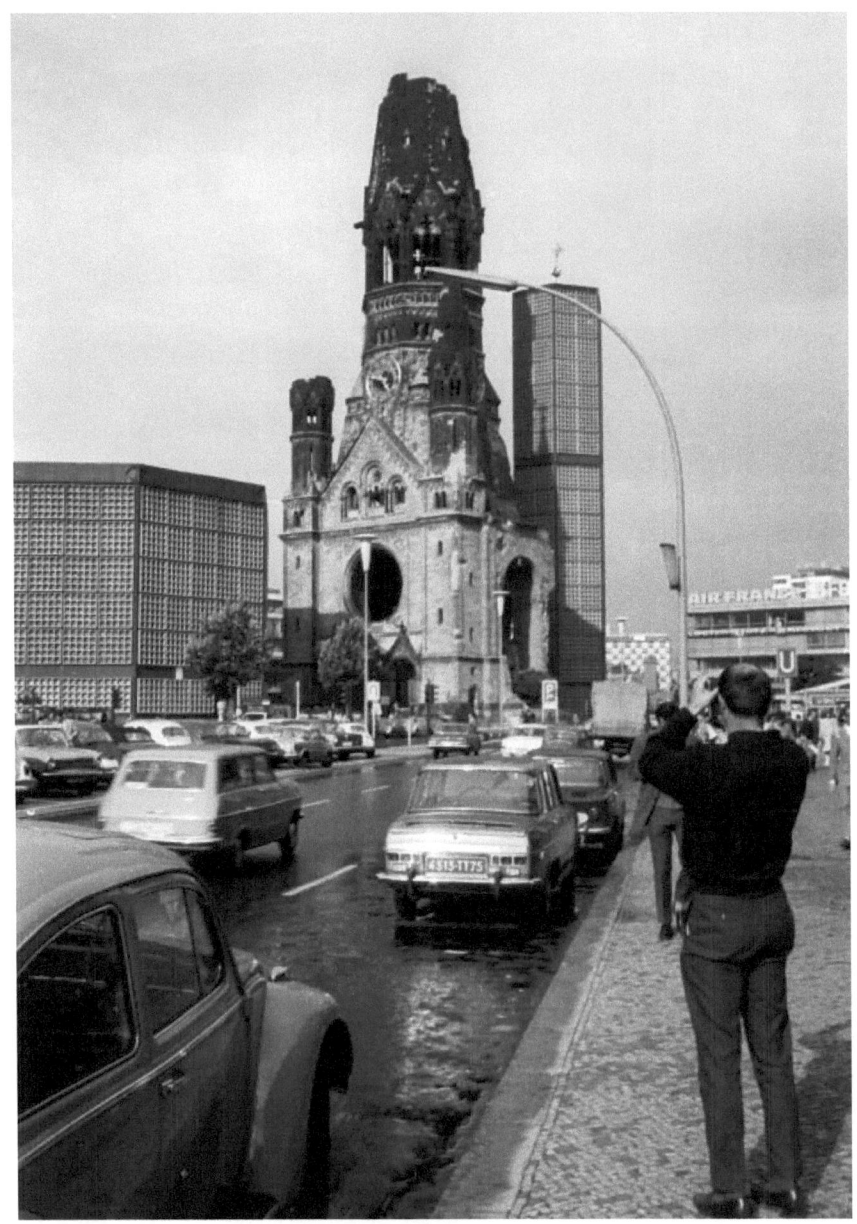

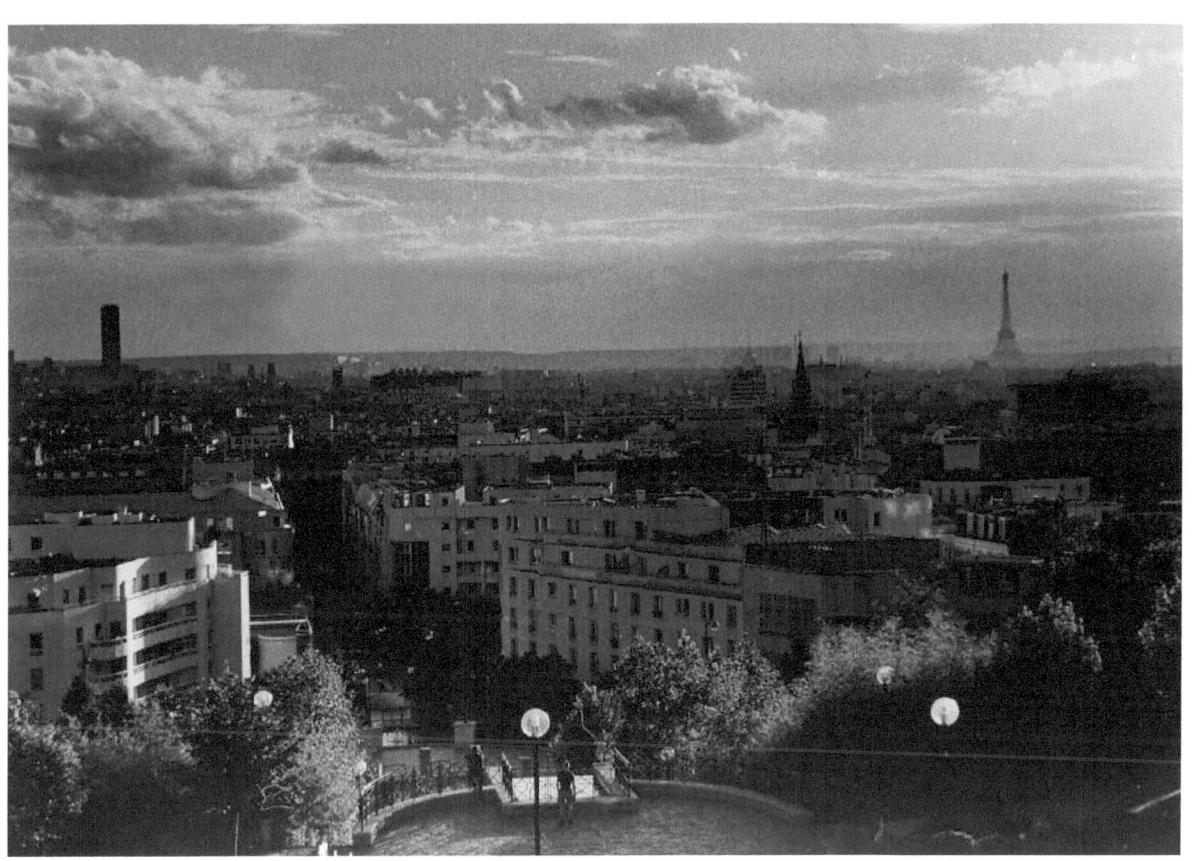

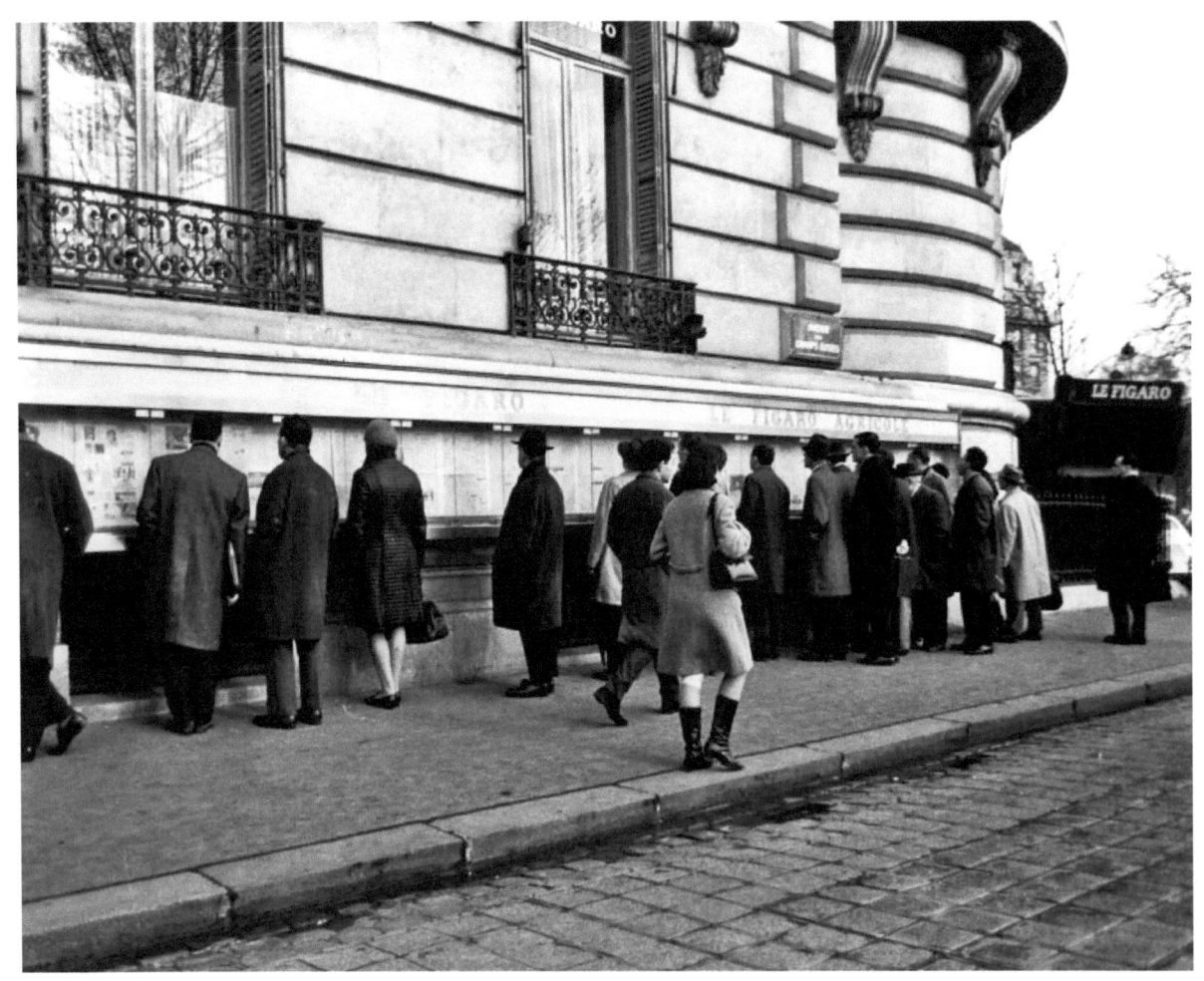

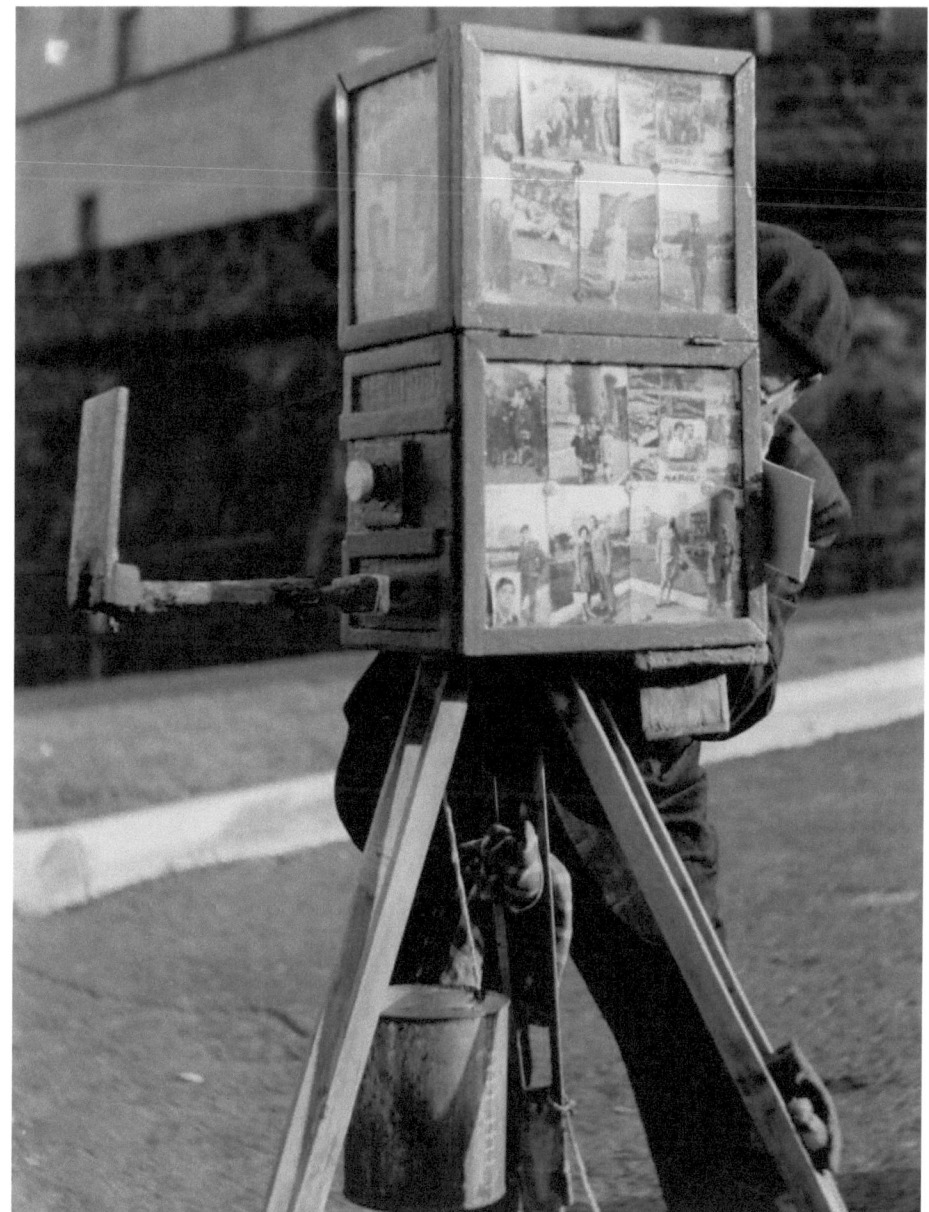

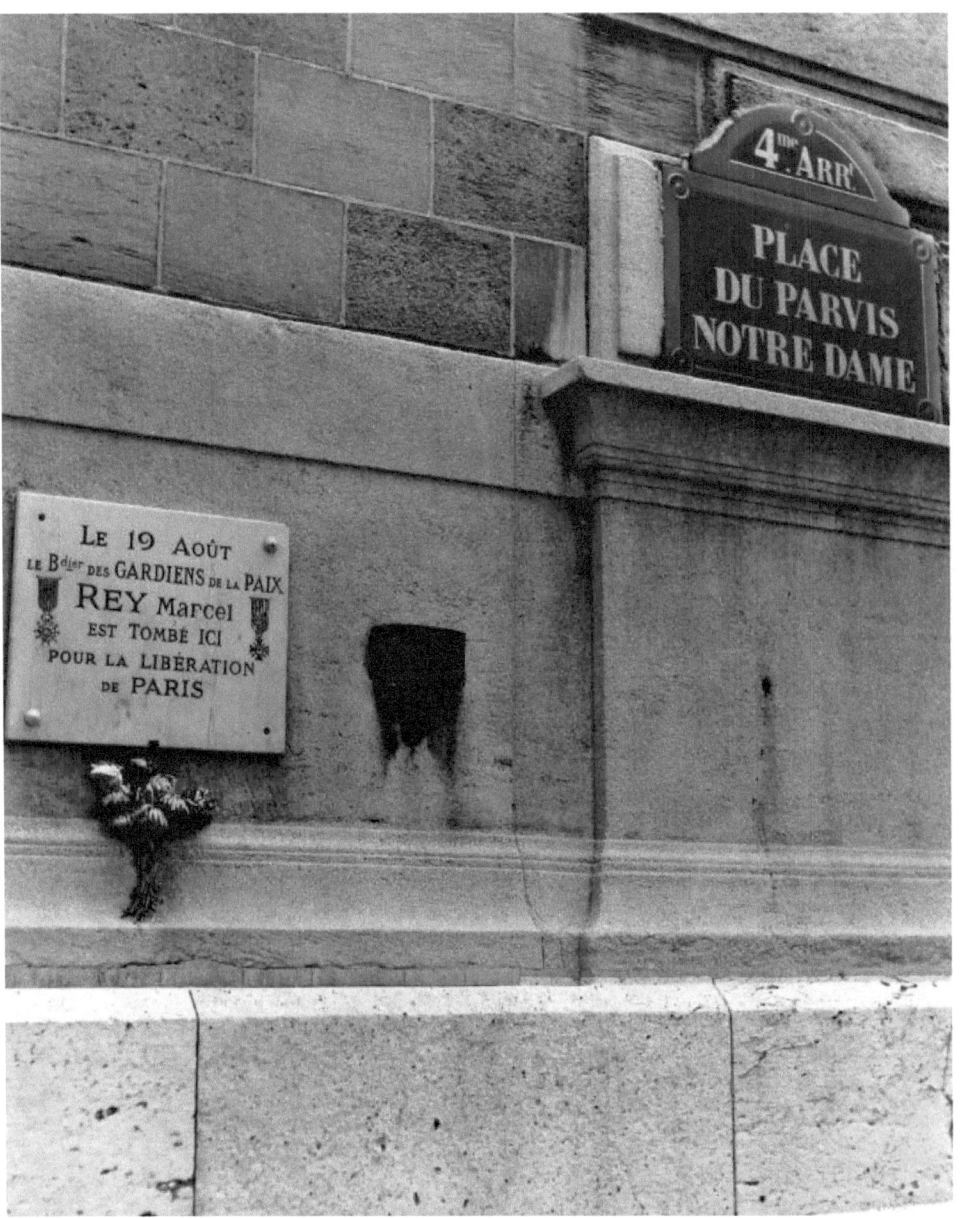

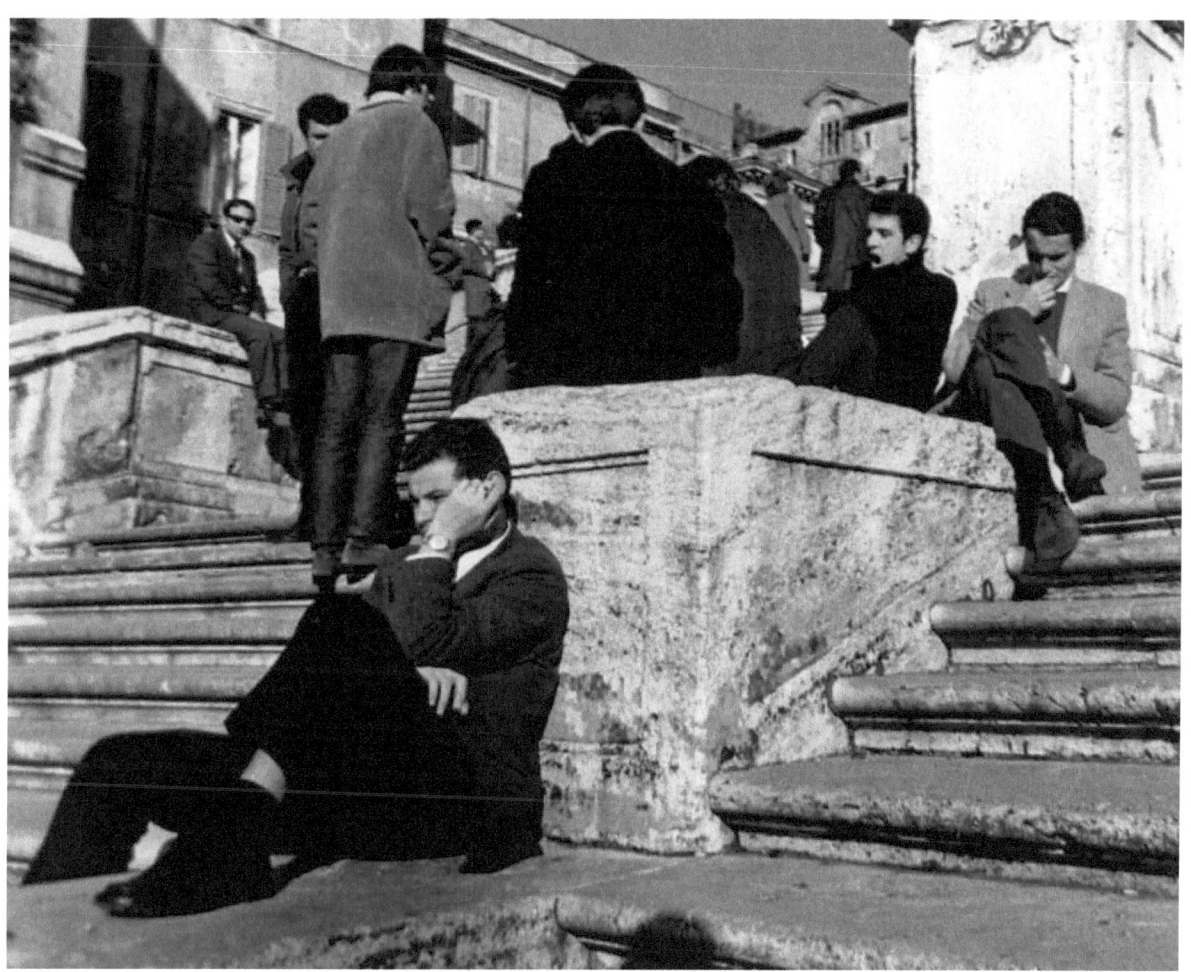

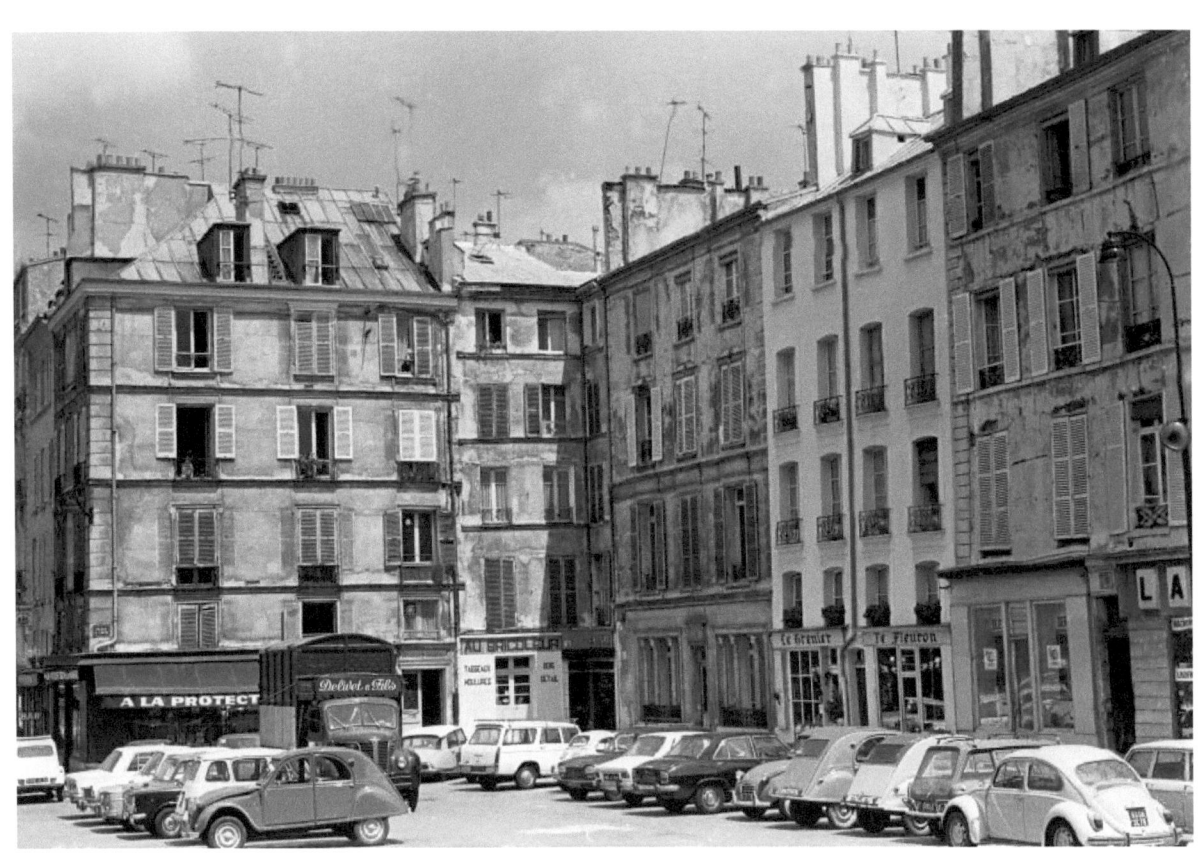

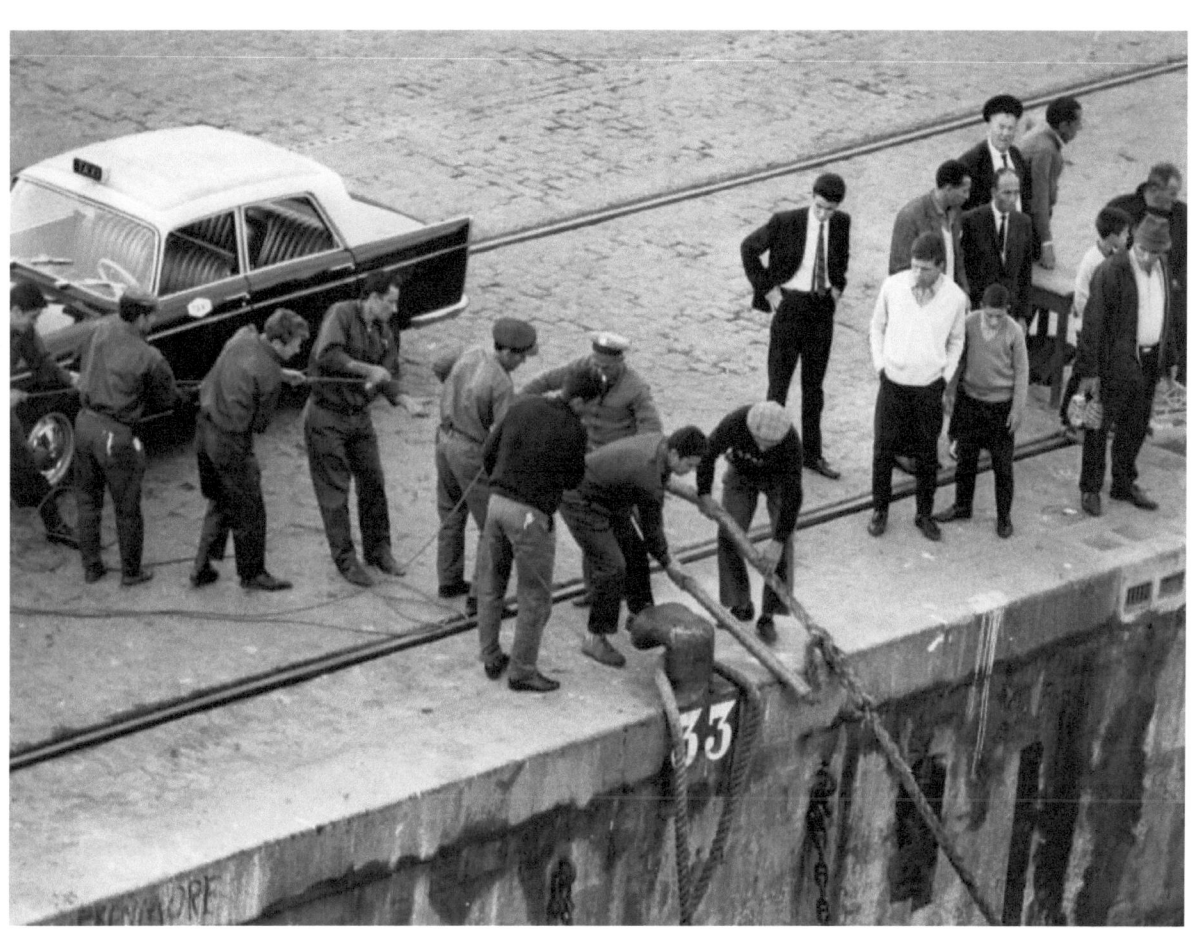

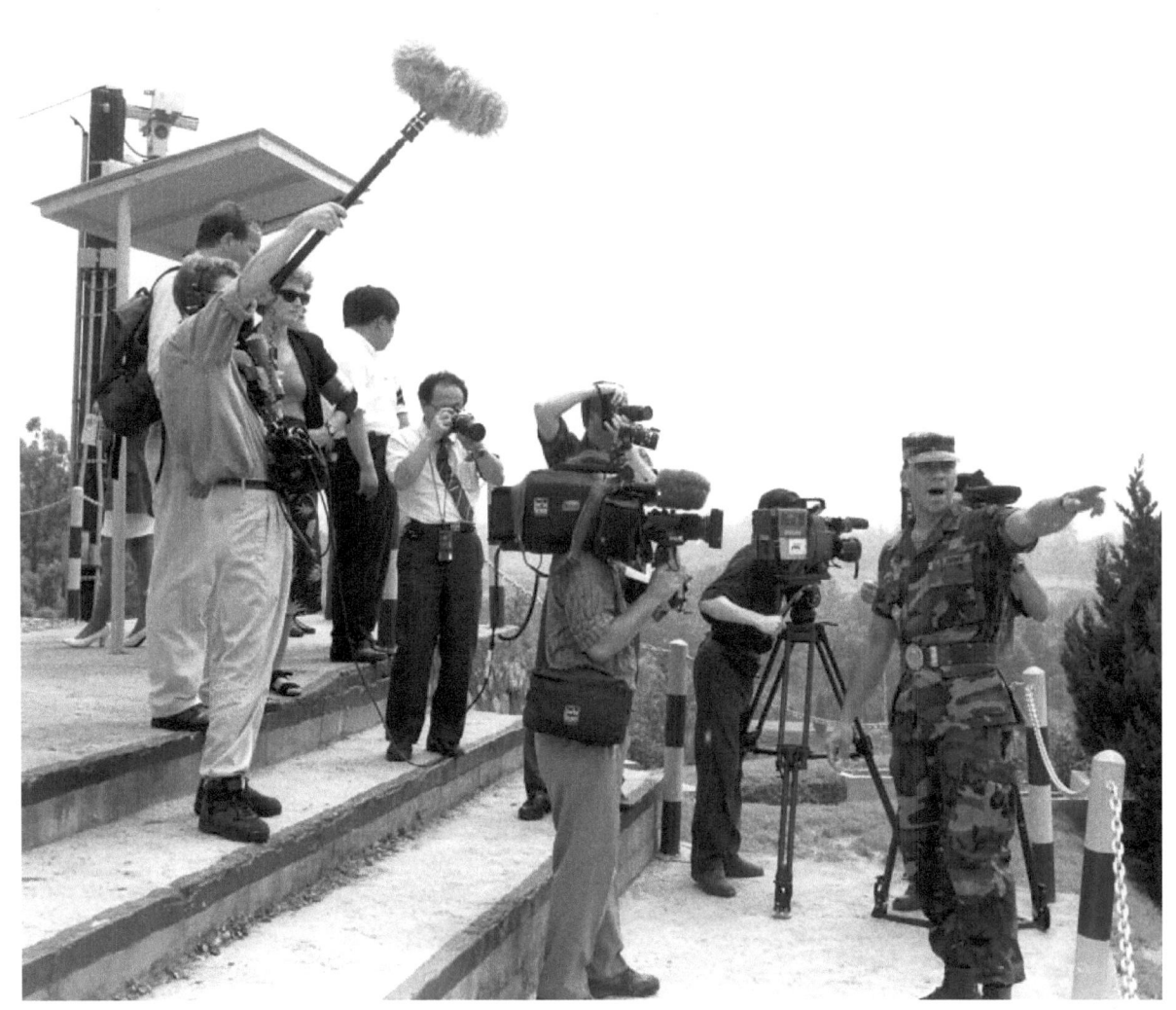

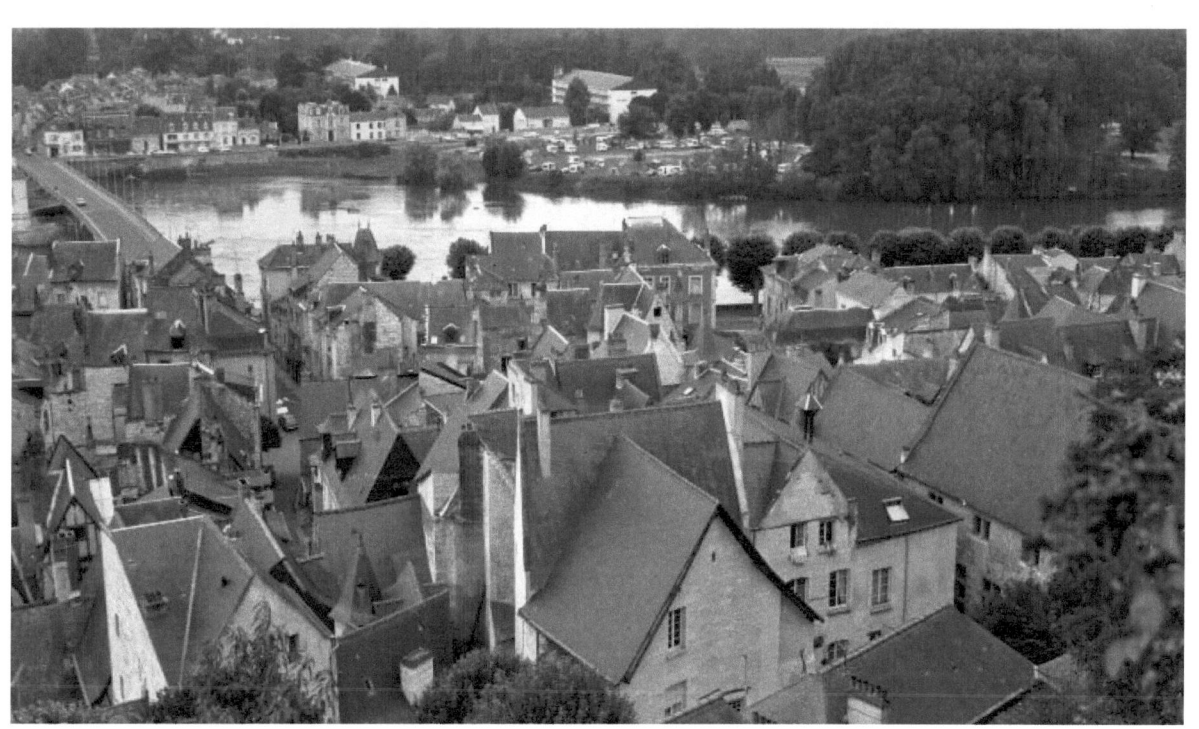

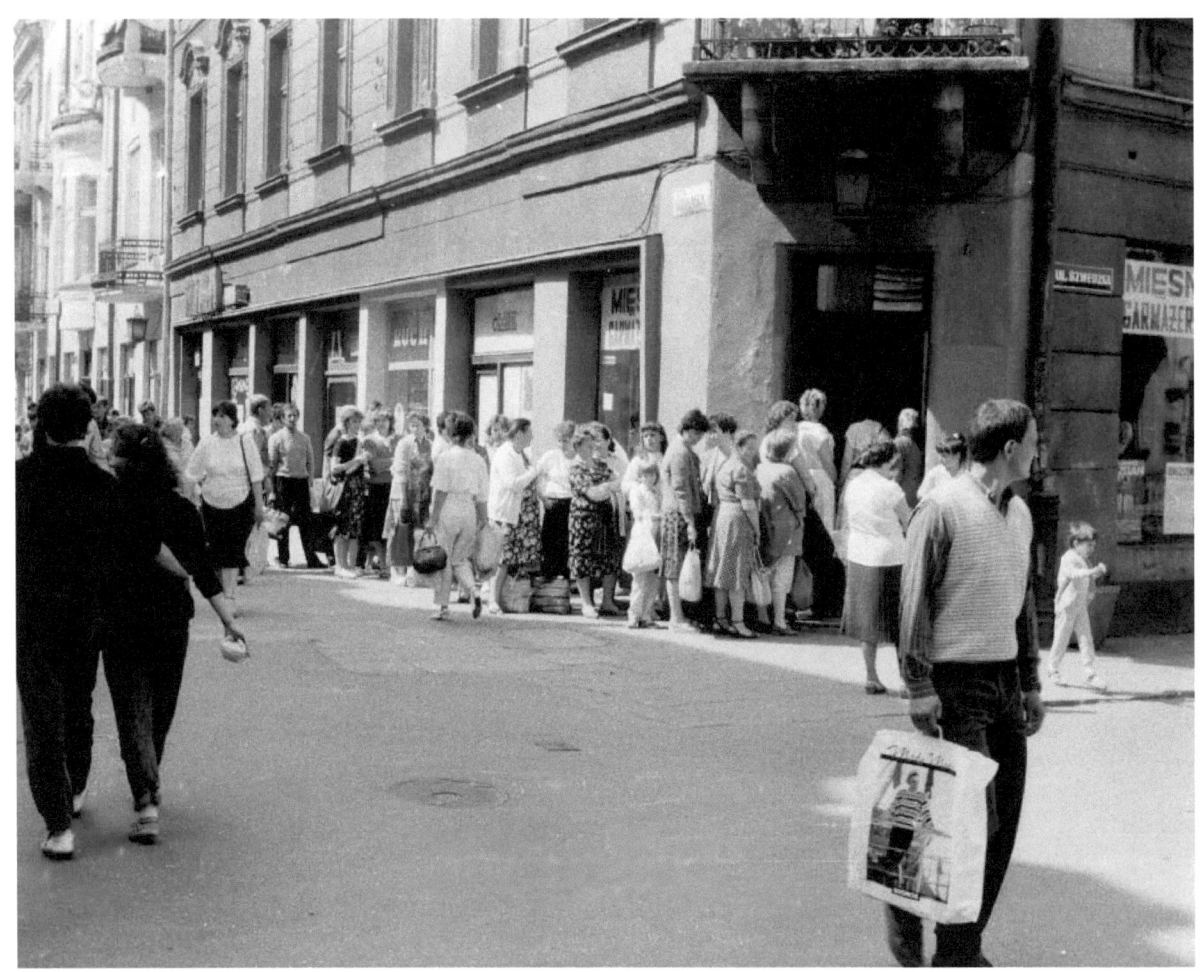

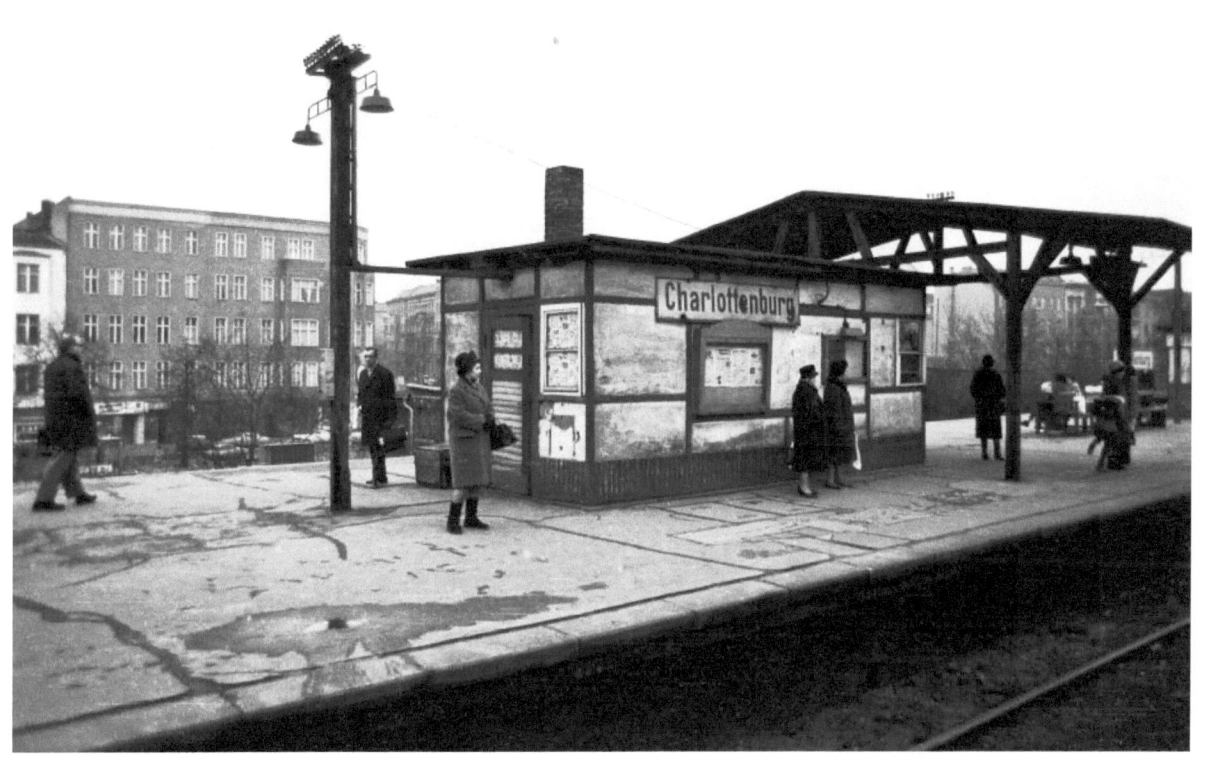

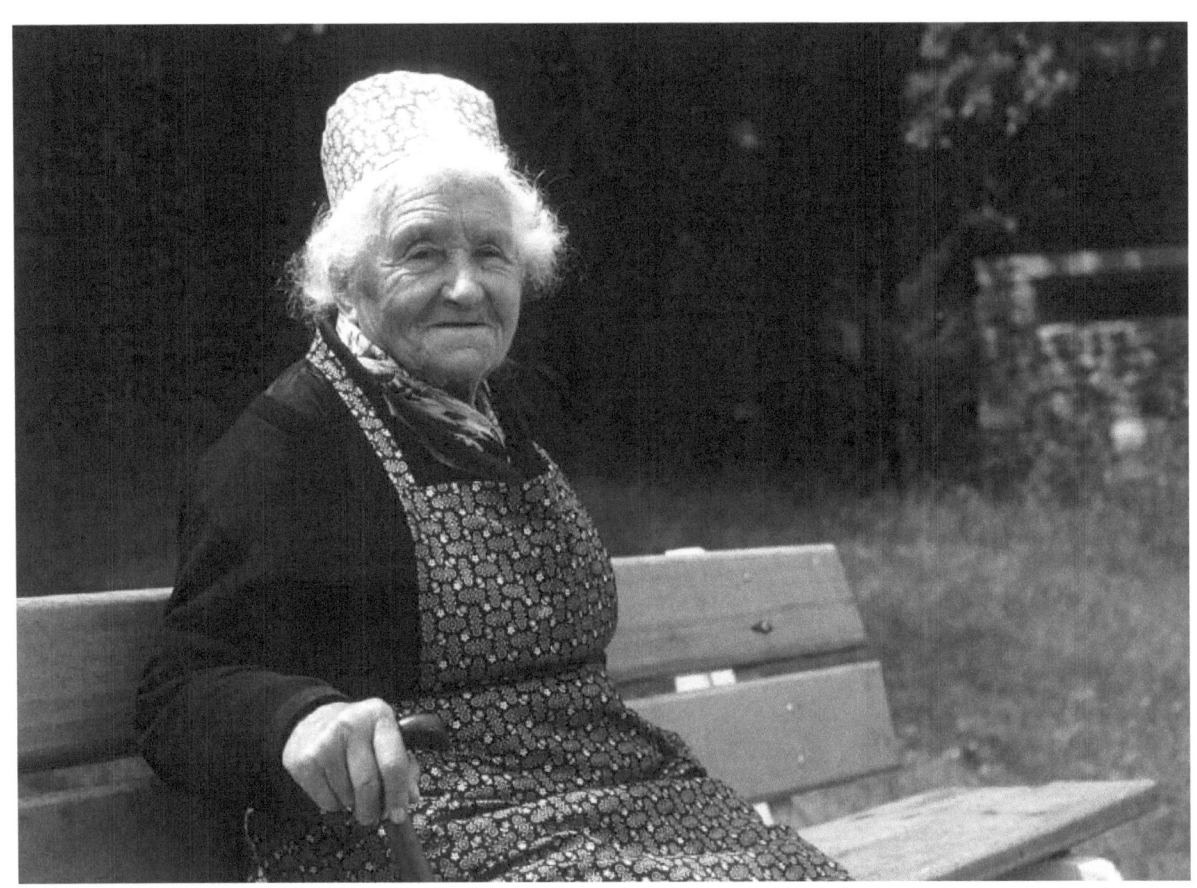

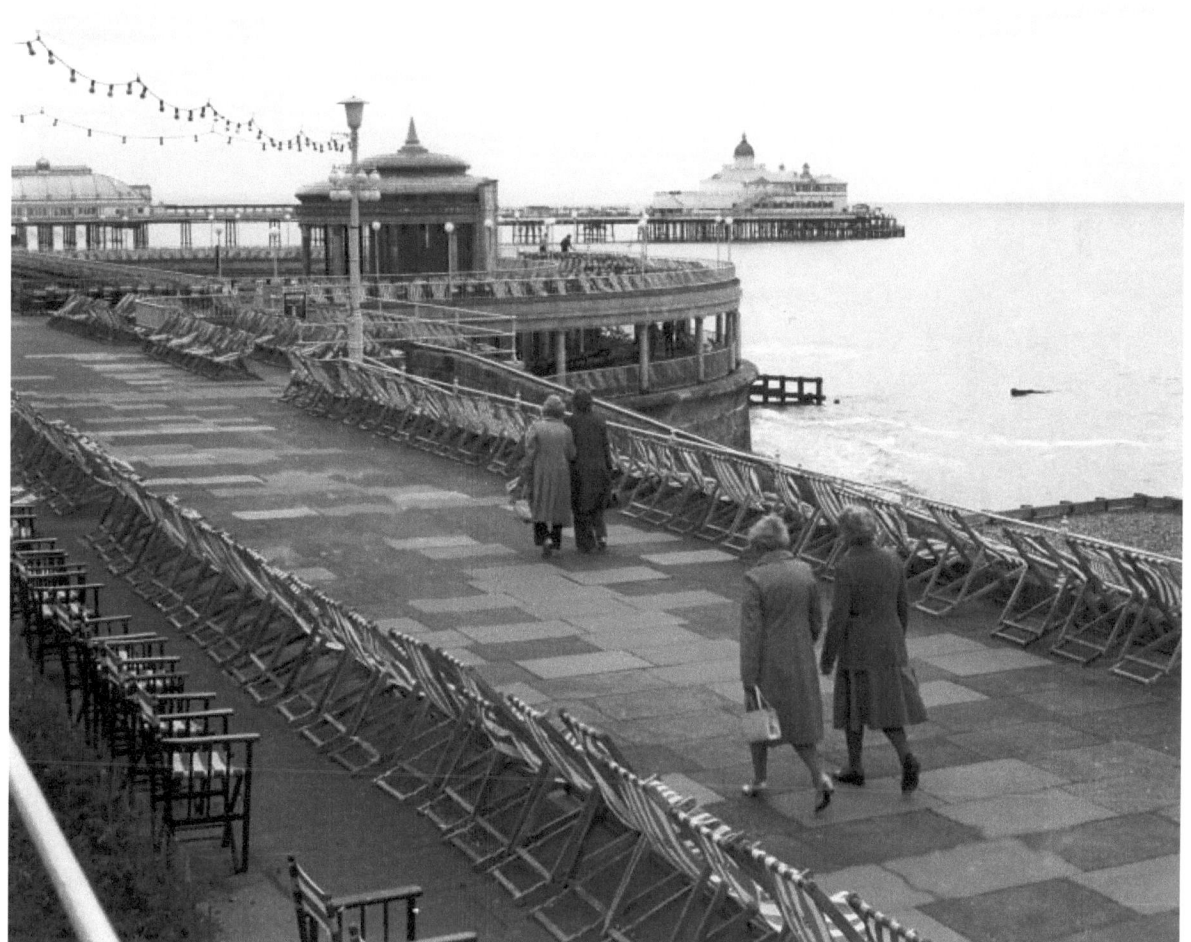

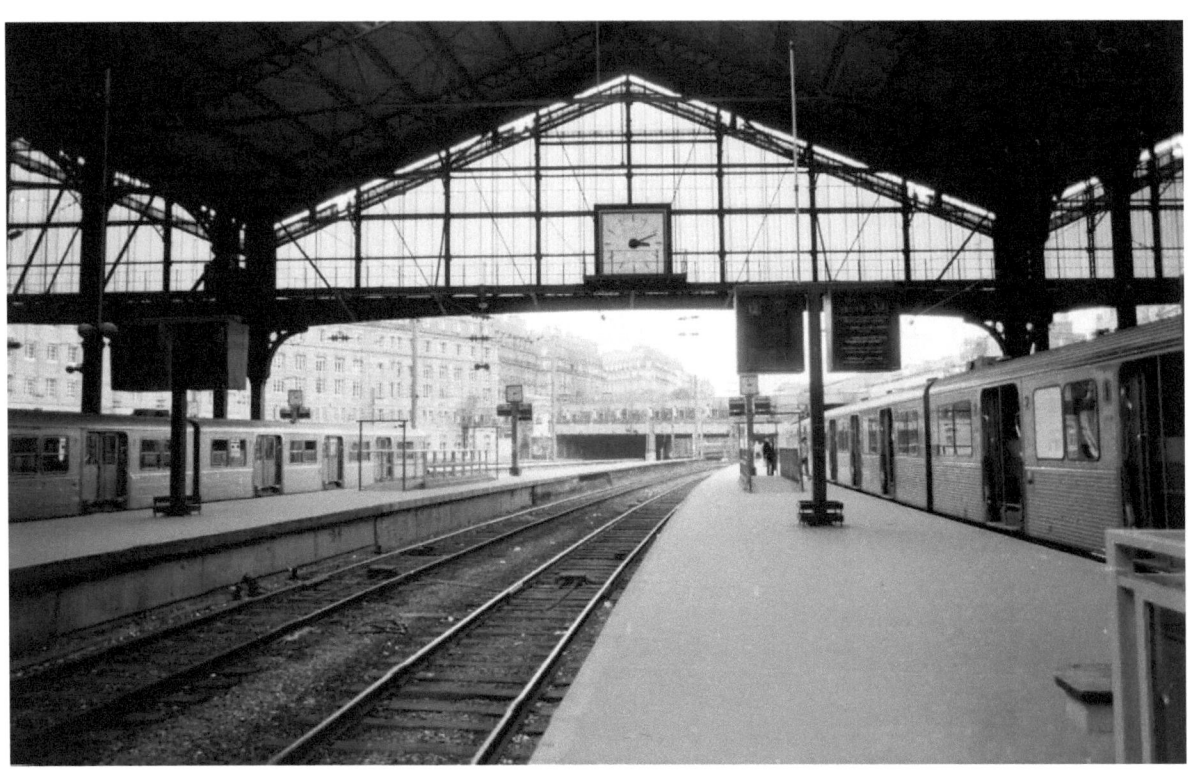

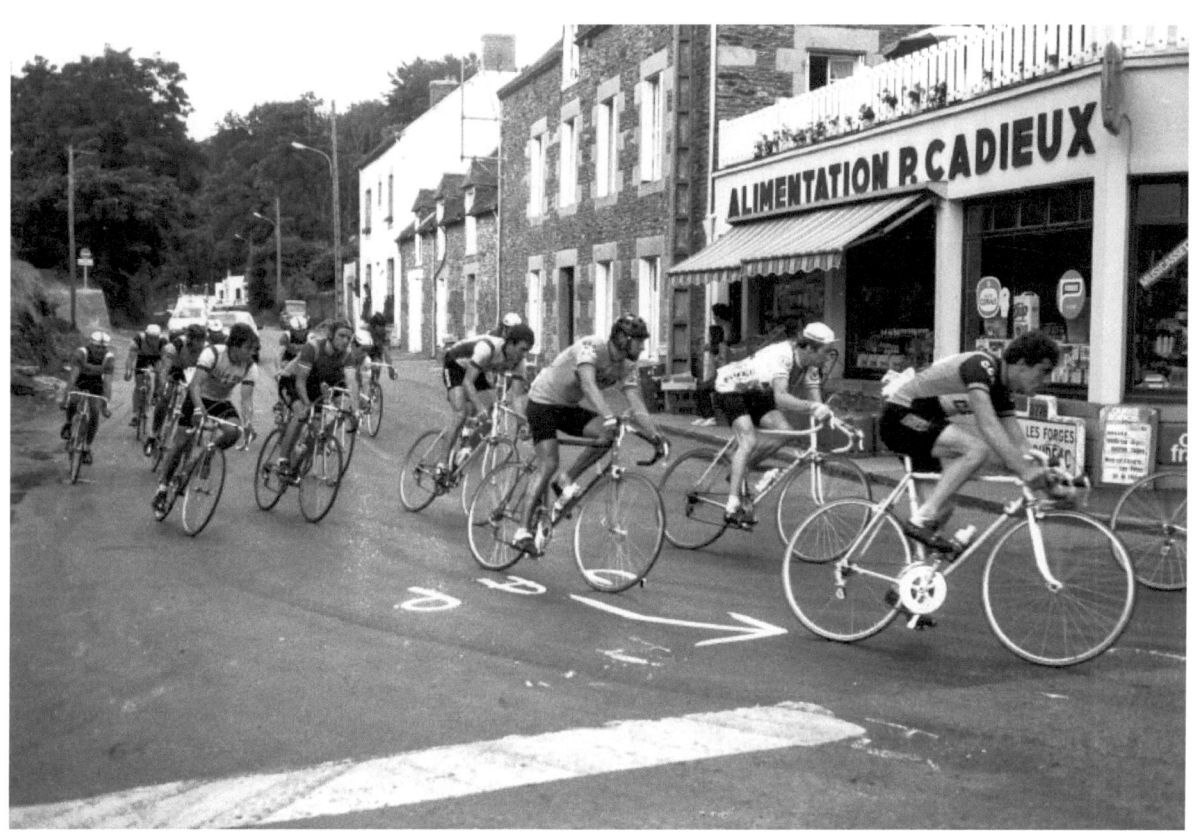

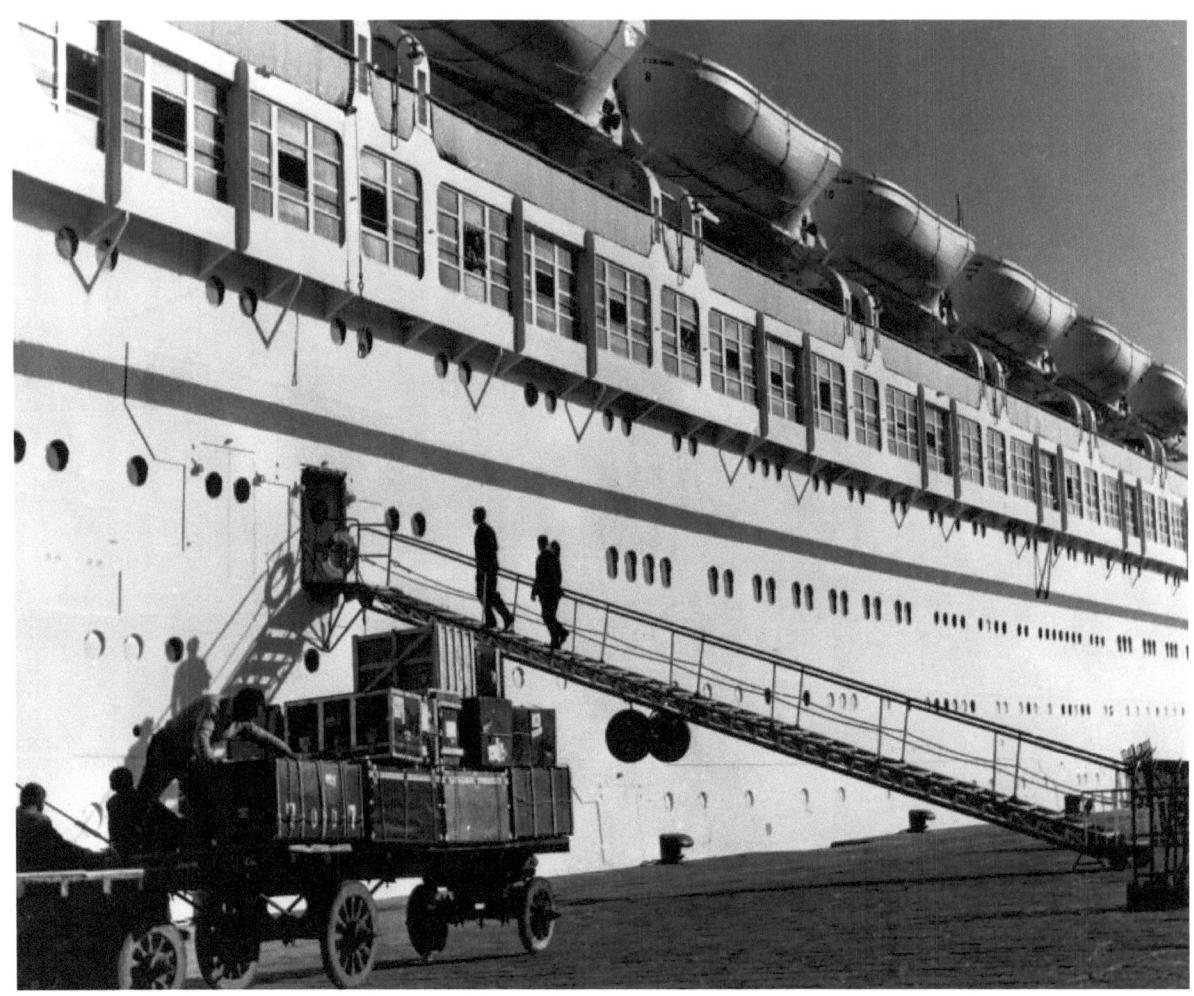

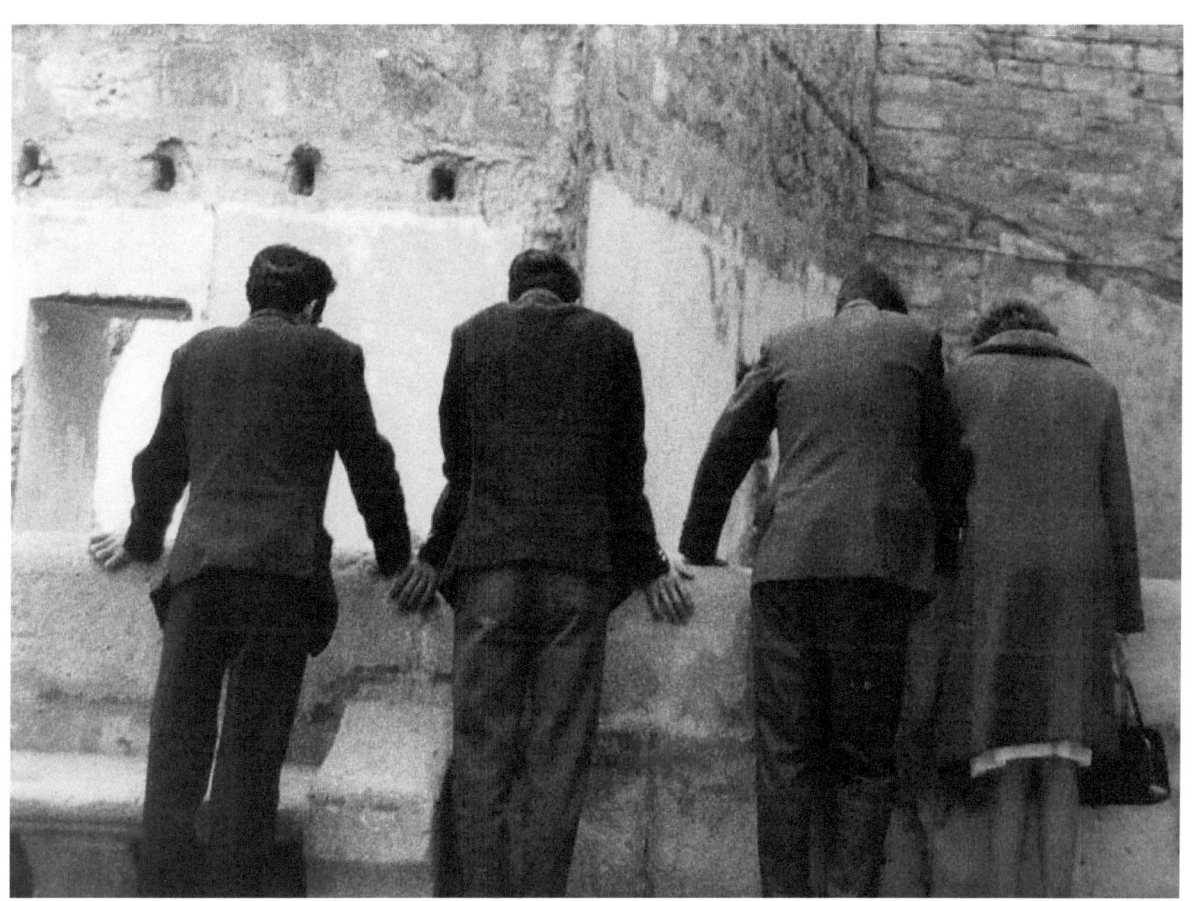

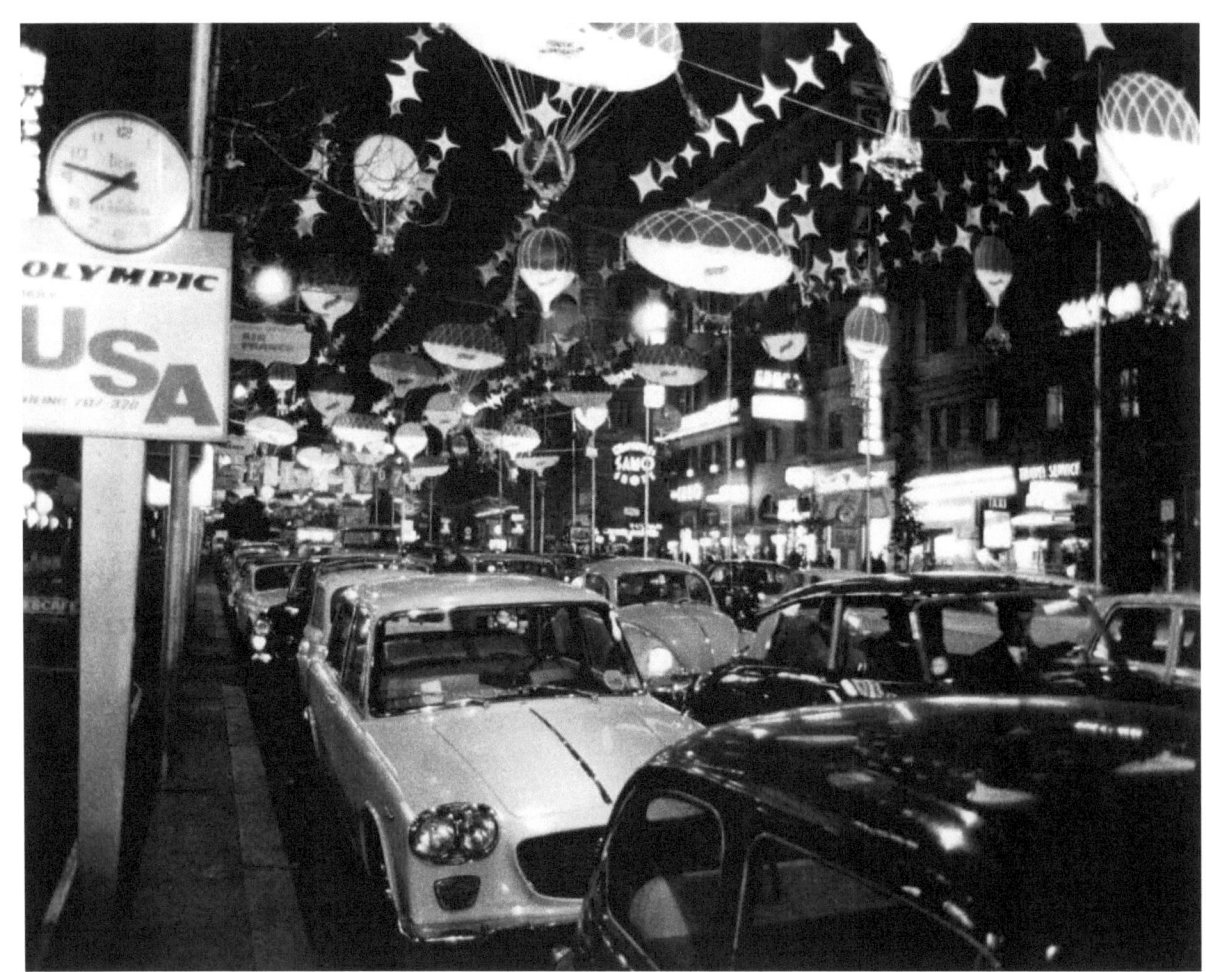

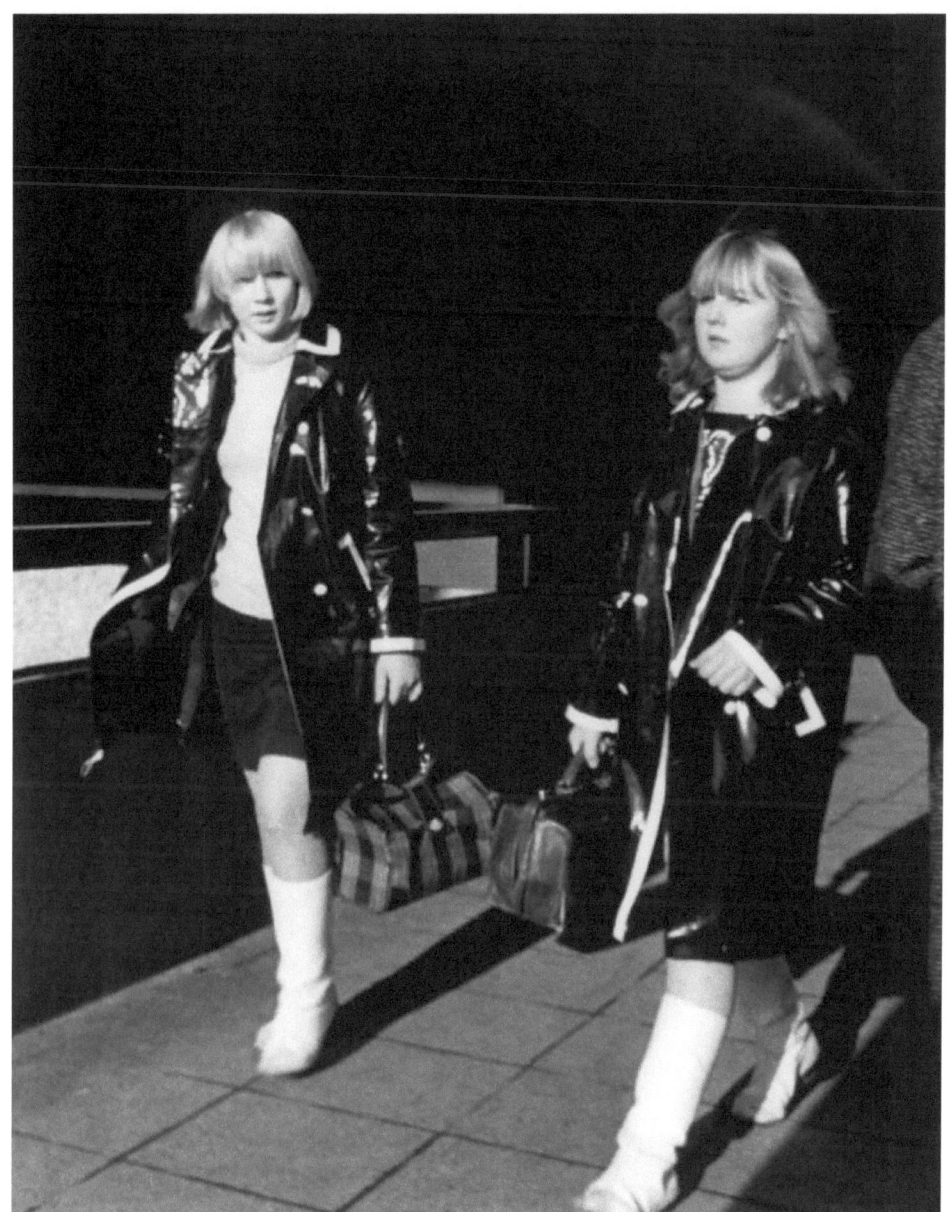

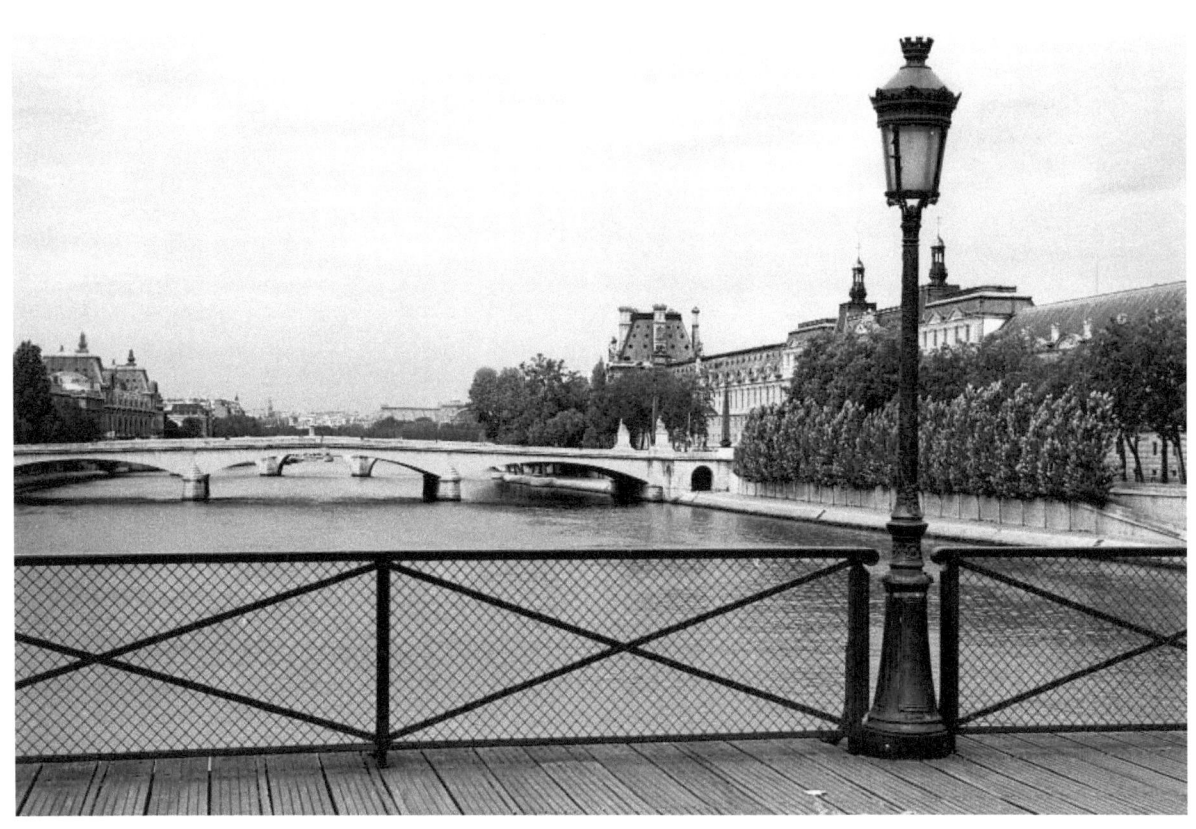

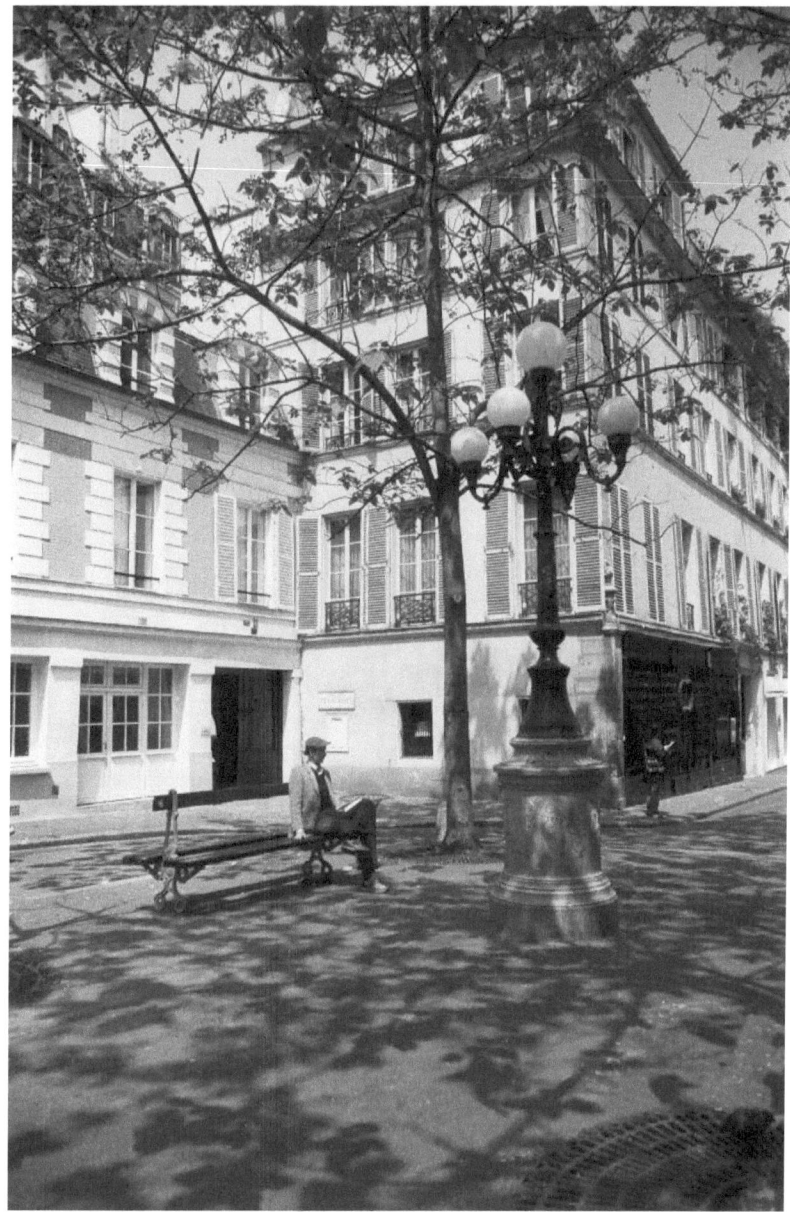

73

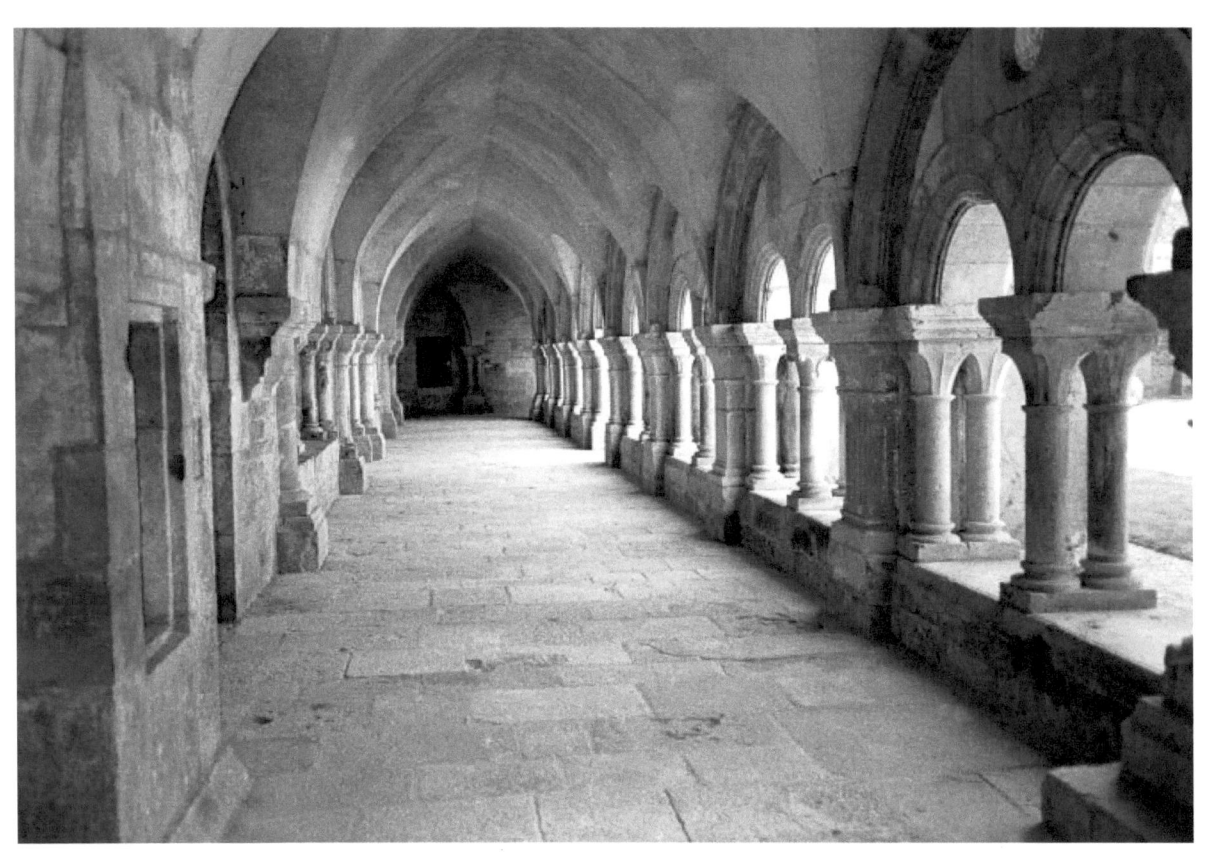

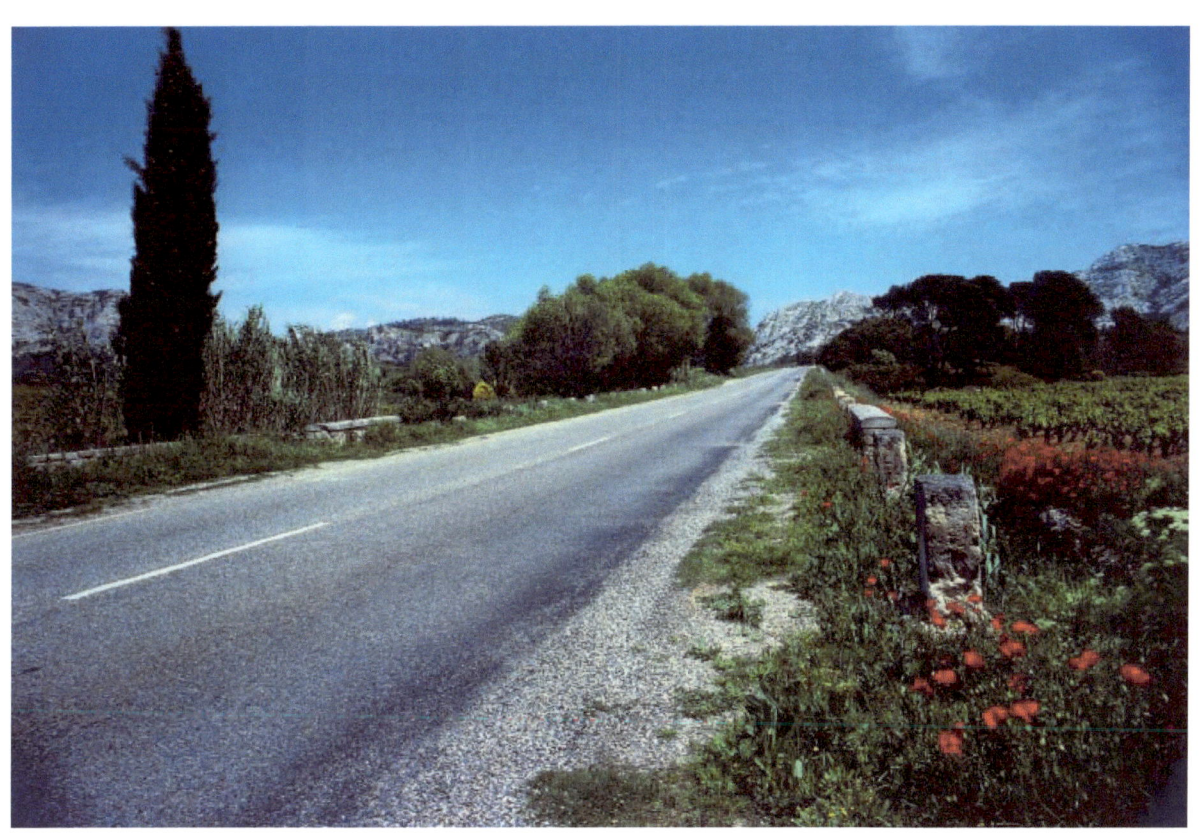

List of photographs

46. Town Square, Nowy Sącz, South Poland

47. Quai d'Anjou, Paris

48. Filling up, Germany, 1950s

49. The infamous Glienecke Bridge which connected West Berlin with East Germany. It is featured in the 2015 film *Bridge of Spies*. Photo taken in 2011.

50. Cemetery, New Orleans, USA

51. Rue Castiglione, Paris

52. The Kaiser Wilhelm Memorial church in former West Berlin, damaged during an air raid in November 1943 and left in that state as a reminder of the war

53. Paris seen from the heights of Belleville

54. At the *Le Figaro* building, Paris

55. Street photographer, southern Europe

56. Tablet commemorating a victim of the 1944 liberation in Paris

57. The Spanish Steps, Rome

58. Fontainebleau, France

59. Helping hands, Madeira

60. TV crews at Panmunjom, South Korea

61. The roofs of Chinon, France

62. People queuing at a butcher's shop, Poland, 1987

63. S-Bahn station, West Berlin, 1950s

64. Woman in Brittany, France

65. At the seaside, England

66. Gare Saint-Lazare, Paris

67. The Tour de France passing through Josselin, Brittany, France, 1981

68. Boarding the ocean liner *Cristoforo Colombo* at Messina, Italy

69. People looking for something, Palma de Mallorca, Spain

Notes on the Photographs

As the title of the book implies, all photographs were taken with analog cameras, ranging from the inexpensive Agfa Silette to more sophisticated gear like Leica and Contarex. Among the cameras were the Olympus Pen half-frame, Rollei 35, Edixa Reflex, Rolleicord, Contarex, Leica M3 and Nikon FE. Film stock was Agfa, Ilford and Kodachrome.

The term 'analog' commonly refers to cameras using film, a method slowly going out of fashion, but this kind of photography still has its followers as the person behind the lens enjoys the pleasures of developing and printing pictures in the darkroom, often in one's bathroom or kitchen.

Although it is convenient to use a digital camera and let your computer and printer do all the work, it seems to take the joy out of hands-on photography.

The mystery of a missing negative, lost in the mail, had to be solved by reproducing the image that I had published in a magazine, and I include it here (page 69).

Wolf Arnold,
Toronto, 2016

www.ingramcontent.com/pod-product-compliance
Lightning Source LLC
Chambersburg PA
CBHW040322190526
45162CB00007B/51